Oh beautiful for halcyon ~~skies~~,
for amber waves of grain,
for purple mountain majesty,
above the enameled plain.

from the 1895 poem "America"
by Katherine Lee Bates

DAVID HISER/ASPEN PHOTOGRAPHERS

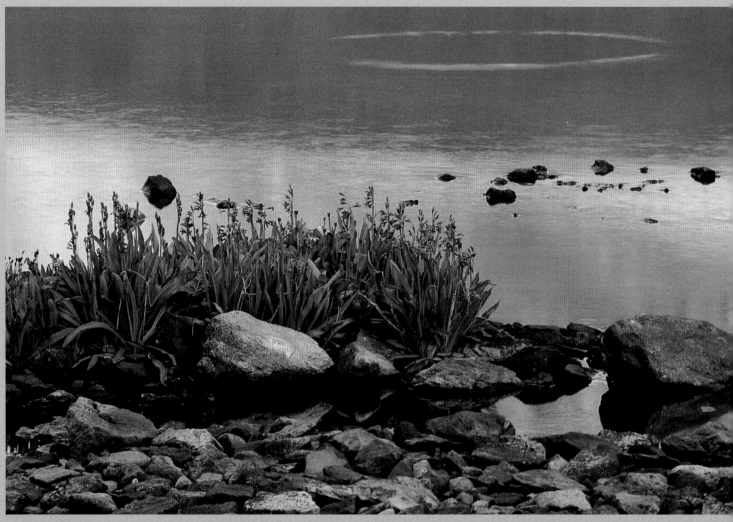

Evening light glows from Fuller Lake, right, in the Ice Lake Basin of the San Juans.
LARRY ULRICH

The San Juans, largest single range in the Rocky Mountains, left, erect a formidable mountain barrier behind this gentle valley. John Charles Fremont called them "one of the highest, most rugged, and impracticable of all the Rocky Mountain Ranges."
LARRY BURTON

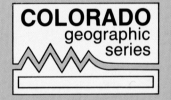

COLORADO
geographic
series

NUMBER TWO
IN THE
COLORADO
GEOGRAPHIC SERIES

BY JEFF RENNICKE

COLORADO
Mountain Ranges

FALCON PRESS

Colorado Geographic Series Staff

Publishers: Michael S. Sample, Bill Schneider
Editor: Russell B. Hill
Photo editors: Michael S. Sample, Bill Schneider
Design: DD Dowden, Bill Schneider
Graphics: Artz-Works of Helena, DD Dowden
Marketing director: Kelly Simmons

Front cover photo

Mount Sneffels, Sneffels Range, Colorado, in autumn. Photo by David Muench.

Back cover photos

"Laying back" in a crack on the "Athlete's Feat" route, Castle Rock, Boulder Canyon, Colorado. Photo by Joe Arnold, Jr.
Bighorn ram. Photo by Michael S. Sample.

For more information

For general information on this book, the Colorado Geographic Series, or other publications of Falcon Press, write Falcon Press, Marketing and Distribution, Box 279, Billings, MT 59103.

In case you missed it . . .

The Rivers of Colorado, book one in the Colorado Geographic Series, is still available. Look for The Rivers of Colorado at your local book dealer. Or to order directly, send $14.95 for softcover or $24.95 for hardcover to Colorado Geographic Series, P.O. Box 279, Billings, Montana 59103. Please include $1.50 per book for postage and handling.

Library of Congress Number: 86-81754
ISBN: 0-934318-66-2 (softcover)
ISBN: 0-934318-92-1 (hardcover)

Design, typesetting, and other pre-press work by Falcon Press, Helena, Montana.

Printed in Japan

STATE OF COLORADO

EXECUTIVE CHAMBERS
136 State Capitol
Denver, Colorado 80203-1792
Phone (303) 866-2471

Richard D. Lamm
Governor

Dear Reader:

Whether you live in Colorado, or travel there in person or through the pages of this volume, you know it is a place of unparalleled beauty and challenge.

I have climbed Colorado's mountains and walked its plains, found the crowds in its cities and found myself, in its most remote reaches. I spend as much time as I can in Colorado's open spaces -- hiking, skiing, climbing, being absorbed by my surroundings.

Colorado offers an exciting variety of topography seldom found in one state -- the plains to the east, the 14,000-foot peaks and the mesas to the west, and the extraordinary Great Sand Dunes.

This book will put you in mind of Colorado's splendor. But I hope you will be moved to place yourself in the midst of it -- come here, and see for yourself what makes Colorado such an extraordinary place.

Richard D. Lamm
Governor

The soft, purple petals of the pasqueflower are often first to break through snow in spring. The flower's name refers to Easter and Passover, the holidays of early spring when the pasqueflower blooms weeks ahead of most other mountain flowers.
MICHAEL S. SAMPLE

Contents

Acknowledgements

Colorado mountains are a big subject. A single lifetime is too short a time to come to know every peak in every range. Many people have helped me in this glimpse of the state's mountain ranges.

Among those I'd like to thank are Dr. Jack Murphy, Curator of Geology at the Denver Museum of Natural History; Dr. Mark Noble of the University of Colorado's Mountain Research Station; Dennis Johns, Director of the Rocky Mountain Biological Laboratory; Dr. James Benedict of the Center for Mountain Archeology; Richard Armstrong of the World Data Center For Glaciology; Mark Udall, the Executive Director of Colorado Outward Bound; Rick Medrick of Outdoor Leadership Training Seminars; Paul Sibley of the International Alpine School; and the staffs of the Carnegie Branch of the Boulder Public Library and the Western History Department of the Denver Public Library.

The skills of the photographers represented in this book bring the beauty of the mountains to light and Russell Hill, the editor, helped to orchestrate the words and pictures.

For the stories, for the inspiration, and for the home-made chokecherry wine, I'd like to thank Carl Blaurock, who in 1923 became the first person to stand atop all of Colorado's 14,000 foot peaks and who today, at 92 years old, still has the far-off look of distant, unclimbed peaks in his eyes. It is people like him that make the mountains of Colorado more than mere rock.

And finally to my wife Jill whose understanding of the clear connection between the beauty of mountains and the grace in pure language is a constant inspiration.

Dedication

Colorado Mountain Ranges is dedicated to my parents, Richard and Carrol Rennicke, for all the mountains, real and imagined, that they helped me to climb.

About the author

Jeff Rennicke is a professional wilderness guide and writer. His work appears in such publications as *Backpacker, Sierra,* and *Wild America* and he is the author of volume one of the Colorado Geographic Series, *The Rivers of Colorado.* As a mountain guide, he has hiked, skied, and camped throughout the mountains of Colorado and currently spends his summers guiding mountain trips in the remote Brooks Range of Alaska. Jeff and his wife Jill live at the foot of the mountains in Lafayette, Colorado.

The mountains of Colorado

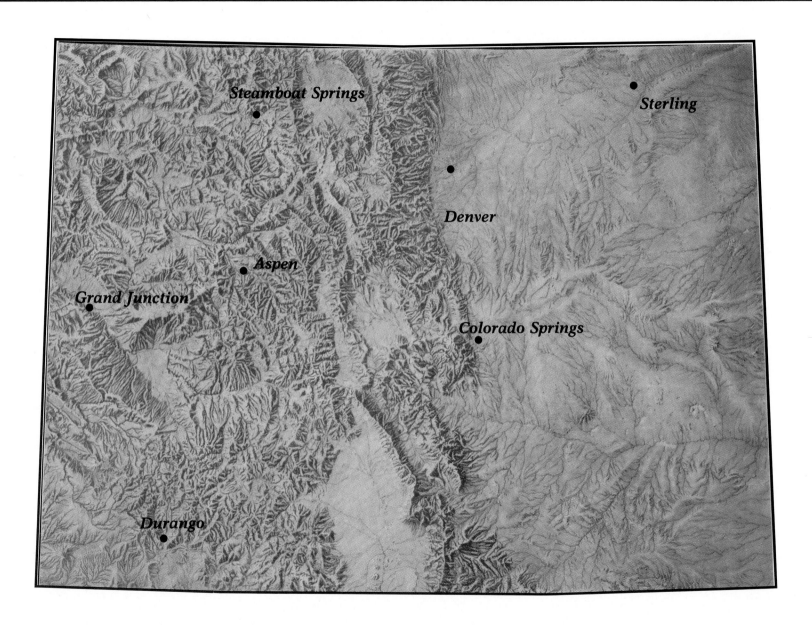

Culebra Range

Elk Mountains

- West Elk Range
- Ruby Range
- Anthracite Range
- Williams Mountains

Elkhead Mountains

- Yampa Williams Fork Mountains

Flattops

Front Range

- Vasquez Mountains
- Tarryall Range
- Platte River Mountains
- Indian Peaks
- Rampart Range
- Kenosha Range
- Laramie Mountains
- Chicago Mountains

Gore Range

Mosquito Range

Mummy Range

Never Summer Range

Park Range

Rabbit Ears Range

Rawahs

Sangre de Cristo Range

- Sierra Blanca Range

San Juans

- La Garita Mountains
- La Plata Mountains
- Sneffels Range
- Needle Mountains
- Grenadiers
- Pico Mountains
- West Needle Mountains
- Piedra Mountains

San Miguel Range

Sawatch Range

- New York Mountains
- Collegiate Peaks

Spanish Peaks

Tenmile Range

Wet Mountains

Williams Fork Mountains

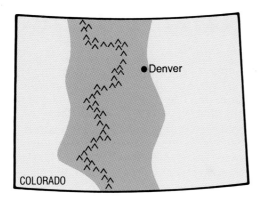

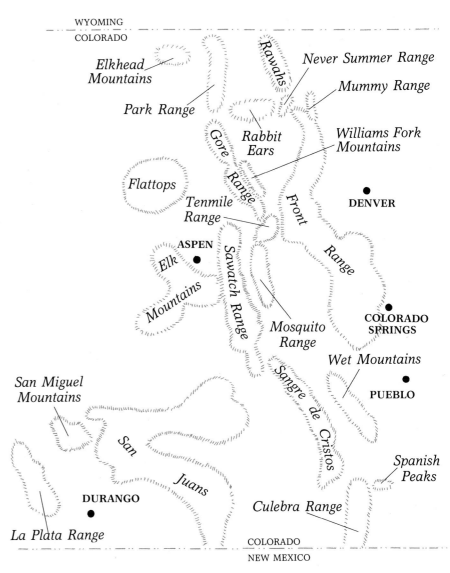

Purple Mountain Majesty

It is an ancient myth that the Rocky Mountains rose out of a stormy primordial sea. Even today, standing atop a peak like Mount Elbert and looking out over the swell of surrounding summits newly dusted with the snow of an early winter storm, it is tempting to imagine the mountains as the tossings of some mythical sea gone to stone.

Mountains have long been makers of myths and weavers of legend. No other facet of the landscape—rivers, canyons, prairies—spawns the range of human emotions which seem to flow off mountains like snowmelt. Like the creeks which carry that snowmelt, these emotions often run deep— so deep that, as Edward Abbey has written, they sometimes "lie closer to music than to words."

People have felt the power of mountains for as long as they have walked the high country. The Utes revered sacred peaks and climbed to them seeking visions, leaving offerings of obsidian and

hand-chipped flints. The mountain men sensed a spirit in the peaks, too, calling them "she" the way sailors refer to ships. And Katherine Lee Bates, a frail professor of English from Wellesley College, recognized that power on a blustery summer day almost a century ago.

On that day in 1895, Bates rode a carriage to a wind-swept summit in the company of Woodrow Wilson. From a spot 14,110 feet into the "spacious skies," Bates looked east across the "fruited plain" and west into a "purple mountain majesty." The power of that mountain touched the poet's soul and so was born a poem and song which touch the depth and breadth of mountain emotions.

The song is "America, the Beautiful." The peak was Pikes Peak in southeastern Colorado. And that "purple mountain majesty" is the heart of the Colorado Rockies.

The Rocky Mountains are the longest mountain

barrier in the world. The chain stretches through three nations from the Alaskan Range through Canada and the U.S. to the Sierra Madre Occidental Range in eastern Mexico. Still, to some, Colorado is the Rockies.

Here the peaks tower to their greatest heights. Mount Elbert in the Sawatch Range reaches 14,433 feet, the highest point in Colorado and the second-highest mountain in the contiguous U.S., trailing only 14,495-foot Mount Whitney in California.

After Mount Elbert, three of the next four highest mountains in the contiguous U.S. reach into Colorado skies and all are within 157 feet of equaling Mount Whitney. Of the 67 U.S. peaks over 14,000 feet, 54 of them are in Colorado. But peaks are measured with more than yardsticks, and human penchant for the biggest and the tallest unfortunately focused attention chiefly on Colorado's 14'ers. Yet, another 830 peaks in the state reach 11,000 feet or more, many of them equally eloquent expressions of mountain beauty. No taller peak in Colorado has lines as graceful as those of Arrow or Vestal peaks in the Grenadiers. No 14,000-foot peak is more difficult or dangerous to climb than the Lizard Head. And no mountain range ever had a more fitting sentry than 12,613-foot Lone Cone. Spirit, not height, is the true measure of mountains.

Colorado has six times more square miles of mountainous country than Switzerland. Even within single ranges, hikers can walk for a month of Saturday nights and still be a hard day's hike from the end of the peaks. The San Juans in the southwest, the largest single range in the Rocky Mountains, occupy more than 10,000 square miles

A full moon shortly after sunset glazes snowy San Juan slopes, left, between Silverton and Ouray.
MICHAEL S. SAMPLE

Rocky Mountain National Park was designated in 1915 as the tenth addition to the National Park System. Sprague Lake, right.
DAVID MUENCH

of mountainous country, about the size of Vermont and part of New Hampshire. Colorado wears wide horizons with an area of 104,247 square miles, much of it in mountains.

The Colorado Rockies are divided into more than fifty ranges and countless peaks, from the Rawahs in the north to the Culebra Range straddling the Colorado-New Mexico border and from Longs Peak on the east to Lone Cone on the west.

The Front Range marks the beginning of Colorado's mountains. After quietly rising more than a vertical mile in a slow, patient gradient from the banks of the Mississippi River to the western edge of the High Plains, the landscape abruptly arches into mountains in one graceful and dramatic swoop. There is nothing timid or indecisive about the way the peaks ambush the long, rolling plains. Travelers from the east can see the Rocky Mountain Front for better than a hundred miles, first appearing on the western horizon as stormclouds, no thicker than shadows or mirages, but gradually materializing to stretch southward like a long, slow, steel-gray freight train.

Millions of people first view the Colorado Rockies this way, from the east. On November 15, 1806, explorer Zebulon Pike, too, first saw the mountain which would bear his name as a "small, blue cloud" on the distant western horizon. The prospectors, mountain men, and settlers who came later and the tourists who come today—for all of them, that darkening of the horizons means they have come upon the Rocky Mountains.

Lost Lake Slough, right, in Gunnison National Forest reflects the sunrise on East Beckwith Mountain. WILLARD CLAY

Columbines bloom below the Three Apostles in the Collegiate Peaks Wilderness, Sawatch Range, far right. JEFF GNASS

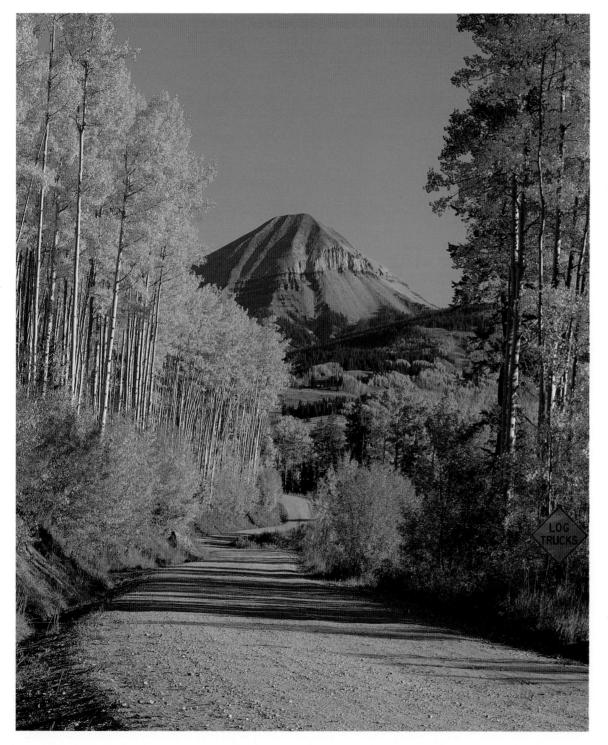

Yet the Front Range is only the start, the shoreline of the sea of peaks in the Colorado Rockies. During the evenings, when the sun goes red, the light streaks through the passes and gaps in the Front Range as if through a door ajar. That door leads to a mountain world, to the isolated Gore Range, to the spectacular Maroon Bells in the Elk Mountains, to the charred, volcanic San Juans, to the Needles slicing and snagging the storm clouds, to the low and wooded Williams Fork Mountains.

These are the mountains of Colorado, the weavers of weather, the makers of myth. Here, some dig for riches like gold or silver. Others come to look, climb, or just sit, gathering a more lasting treasure. Peaks become cornerstones, landmarks in a personal landscape for those who live in these mountains. And for those who visit, the memory of an ice-gray peak gone gold with sunset becomes a similar kind of touchstone. Mountains are like that.

Sitting atop Pikes Peak on such an evening, watching the sunset across the mountains, the light still settles like waves on an ancient ocean, going gold like the aspen in autumn, going white the color of frost, going red and sometimes, when the light strikes just exactly right, even going a deep shade of purple, just like it says in the song. ■

Engineer Mountain, left, in the San Juans stands 12,968 feet and yet is dwarfed by nearby peaks. RENE PAULI

An autumn snowstorm in the Elk Range, right, highlights the colorful designs of aspen in Maroon Creek Canyon. JEFF GNASS

Page 14: Winter begins to loosen its grip on Ice Lake in the San Juans. LARRY ULRICH

Page 15: Today, the Great Sand Dunes Monument in the southwestern corner of the Sangre de Cristos preserves a unique ecosystem in one of Colorado's driest areas. STEPHEN TRIMBLE.

A rainbow of life

In the valley, it is springtime. The creek hums with the satisfaction of fullness. Monkeyflower and saxifrage bloom along its banks, and aspen on the hillsides are hazy with new leaves.

But in the high country, winter still has its claws dug deep. Even though the sun hits the highest peaks first each morning, its light glints off the snow unbroken except where wind has exposed bare rock. Nothing moves, nothing blooms.

Mountains confuse the simple order of the seasons. In the Colorado Rockies, a rise of 1,000 feet in elevation approximates a 600-mile journey to the north. As elevation increases, average temperature decreases, snowpack deepens, the growing season shortens, sunlight becomes more intense, and winds blow harder.

In the Sangre de Cristo Range where peaks tower 6,000 feet above valleys, or in the Front Range, or on the slopes of other peaks which rise more than a mile above their surroundings, spring flowers bloom in valleys while snow squalls gather on summits. Between the blooming flowers and the snowstorms, seasons blend like the colors of a rainbow, creating a mosaic of life. Every step up the mountainside brings changes, however slight—the dry brown of an autumn prairie, the deep green of Douglas fir, the blue of reflected sky in a cirque lake, the red and orange splashes of lichen, and the soft white of snow.

Every gust of wind or passing snowcloud creates an advantage for one species or puts another at the limits of its range. Plant and animal species claim territories where conditions allow a foothold. Where the conditions change, even a little, new plants spring up, the tracks of new animals appear, and ecosystems meet, blend, and overlap, just like the colors of the rainbow.

Thus, mountains, in a sense, compress distance—by mirroring differences in latitude (measured in thousands of miles) with differences in altitude (measured in thousands of feet). In 1890, while collecting plant specimens in the San Francisco Peaks in Arizona, Dr. C. Hart Merriam first came upon this power of mountains to compress distance.

A double rainbow seems to halo this bristlecone pine left, on Mt. Evans in the Front Range. Bristlecone pines, pinus aristata, *are among the longest-living things on earth, with one tree dating back 4,600 years. Colorado's oldest bristlecone pines probably sprouted about the time of Christ, and owe their amazing longevity to the retention of needles for thirty years and more, a dense cellular structure which retards insect damage and decay, and the ability to produce seeds when only 10 percent of their tissue is living. TIM LUCAS*

Wild daisies accent this lush garden, right, in the Maroon Bells- Snowmass Wilderness. CARR CLIFTON

Climbing through various altitudes of Arizona peaks, Merriam observed plants and animals usually associated with the forests of Canada. From the highest summits, he collected species common to arctic regions far north. It was as if the species had been forced south by the most recent glacial period and later—as those glaciers retreated—had become "stranded on mountains," as Merriam put it.

The concept of life zones was, even before Merriam's day, an accepted scientific doctrine. But until Merriam recognized the role of elevation, life zones and their boundaries had been explained only in terms of latitude. Tropical species, everyone knew, grew in lower latitudes near the equator; temperate species flourished in the milder climates of the middle latitudes; higher latitudes saw the hardwoods slowly give way to dark coniferous forests of the north; and finally trees gave way altogether at arctic latitudes. By calling attention to the succession of species on mountainsides, however, Merriam demonstrated that vegetation zones were determined by elevation as well as latitude.

Few places in the world have within their borders the range of elevation found in Colorado. Its highest point, the summit of Mount Elbert in the Sawatch Range, stands at 14,433 feet. The lowest point in the state, along the banks of the Arkansas River where it crosses into Kansas near the town of Holly, is only 3,350 feet above sea level.

The difference—the height of Colorado measured from head to toe—is 11,083 feet, more than two vertical miles. Using the "600 miles/1000 feet" formula, that means that a kayaker on the Arkansas River who climbed to the summit of Mount Elbert would encounter changes in vegetation and climate similar to those he would encounter on a trip from the southern plains to the Arctic Circle.

Compressed into those two vertical miles of

Tucked high in the state's mountains, fragile wetlands like this alpine pool, right, near the Molas Divide in the San Juans reflect the sky and create conditions favorable for plant species found nowhere else in the mountains. The resulting diversity of plantlife provides important food, cover, and habitat for animal species, making the wetlands perhaps the mountain's most fertile ecosystem.
DAVID MUENCH

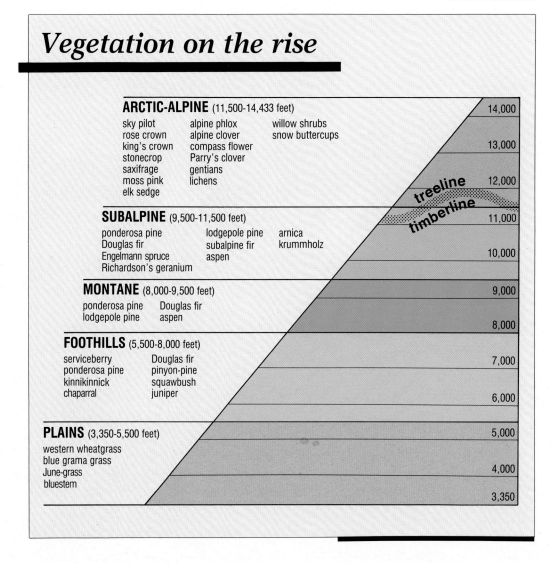

Vegetation on the rise

ARCTIC-ALPINE (11,500-14,433 feet)

sky pilot	alpine phlox	willow shrubs
rose crown	alpine clover	snow buttercups
king's crown	compass flower	
stonecrop	Parry's clover	
saxifrage	gentians	
moss pink	lichens	
elk sedge		

SUBALPINE (9,500-11,500 feet)

ponderosa pine	lodgepole pine	arnica
Douglas fir	subalpine fir	krummholz
Engelmann spruce	aspen	
Richardson's geranium		

MONTANE (8,000-9,500 feet)

ponderosa pine	Douglas fir
lodgepole pine	aspen

FOOTHILLS (5,500-8,000 feet)

serviceberry	Douglas fir
ponderosa pine	pinyon-pine
kinnikinnick	squawbush
chaparral	juniper

PLAINS (3,350-5,500 feet)
western wheatgrass
blue grama grass
June-grass
bluestem

treeline
timberline

14,000
13,000
12,000
11,000
10,000
9,000
8,000
7,000
6,000
5,000
4,000
3,350

relief in Colorado are five major life zones—the Plains (3,350-5,500 feet), Foothills (5,500-8,000 feet), Montane (8,000-9,500 feet), Subalpine (9,500-11,500 feet), and Arctic-Alpine (11,500-14,433 feet).

None of these zones, of course, are separated by white boundary lines painted across the mountains of the state. The elevations listed above are, at best, general guidelines based upon the eastern slope of the Colorado Rockies, where most research has been conducted. Altitudes of zones on the western slope typically are higher because of increases in precipitation. For instance, the Subalpine zone, reaching only 11,000 feet in dry northeastern ranges like the Rawahs, climbs as high as 12,000 feet in southwestern mountains like the Needles.

Other factors besides east-west location have an impact on life zones. South-facing slopes, for instance, are exposed to more intense sunlight for greater periods of time than north-facing slopes. Consequently, southern slopes hold less snow, heat up and dry out more quickly, and have longer growing seasons. Such slopes can extend the range of low-elevation species upwards as much as 2,000 feet. On the other hand, cold, damp, north-facing slopes allow high-altitude species to descend into lower elevations.

Within the major life zones, still smaller zones known as ''micro climates'' exist—mountain streams; the harsh environment of talus slopes; avalanche paths stubbled with aspen; areas temporarily disturbed by rock slides, fires, or even

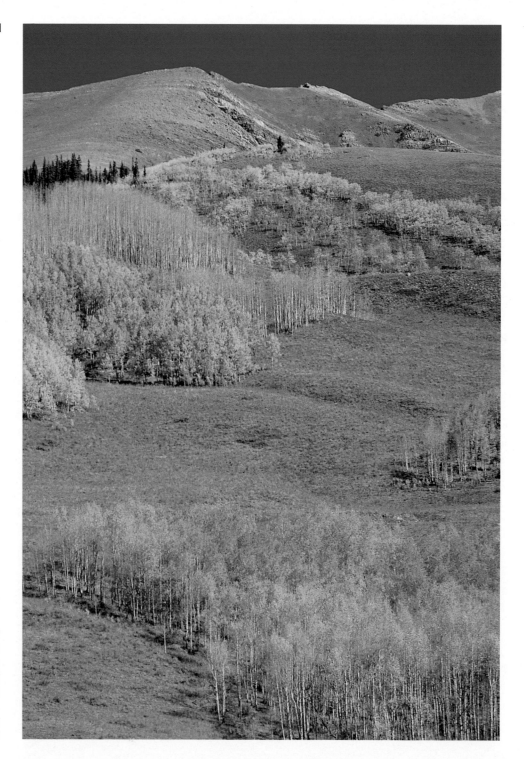

As these groves in the East River Valley vividly illustrate, aspen often sprout from a common root system and thus individual trees within groves closely resemble each other, sprouting new leaves in spring and turning colors in autumn within a few days of each other. Meanwhile, adjacent groves display striking differences of color. DENNIS W. JOHNS

Even in summer, ice-bound willows, above, serve as frequent reminders that winter is never far off.
MICHAEL S. SAMPLE

Just as the bugling of bull elk signals autumn, the calving of cow elk, above, signals spring. With winter snows melting off the peaks, cow elk gather on traditional calving grounds to drop their young before moving higher into the mountains for summer.

At the turn of the century, elk had almost disappeared. Unregulated hunting, destruction of winter range and calving grounds, competition for forage from domestic herds, and unwise management practices reduced numbers of elk not just in Colorado but across the nation.

Transplants from healthier herds across the West stabilized the numbers of elk. Later, strict hunting regulations and designation of important calving and wintering grounds helped Colorado's herds grow into one of the largest elk populations in North America.
MICHAEL S. SAMPLE

human activities like logging, road-building, and the introduction of non-native species. The concept of life zones is simply not the tidy system it was once thought to be. Instead, each mountain is a collage of events and forces waiting to happen.

In the Shadow of Mountains

The Colorado plains might seem an unlikely beginning for Colorado's mountains. But the plains wind, just like the gales that slice the air above timberline, cuts as sharply as shattered ice. The stars have the same clarity and the darkness shares the same silence as in the high places.

The power of mountains extends far beyond their rocks, farther even than their shadow. In his book *American Indians in Colorado*, J. Donald Hughes describes the mountain Utes hunting ''as far out onto the plains as the shadows of the Rockies stretch at sunset.'' But the Colorado Rockies cast another shadow across the plains which has nothing to do with sunsets.

Prevailing westerly winds pit heavy, moisture-laden clouds from the Pacific Ocean against the mountains of Colorado. To cross the Rockies, those winds must rise, cool, and drop their precipitation. By the time they drift over the eastern plains, the prevailing winds have been wrung dry, leaving little rain or snow for the plains. This ''rain shadow'' cast by the Colorado Rockies causes striking differences in precipitation levels within short distances. For example, winter buries Cumbres Pass in the southeastern San Juans, one of the snowiest spots in Colorado, with 370 inches of snow each winter. Yet, just thirty miles east, the town of Manassa in the San Luis Valley is as dry as a rusty bucket, averaging only seven inches of precipitation annually.

Because of the heavy toll they exact from eastbound weather, Colorado's mountains influence everything that lives on the plains below them. The glaring sun is rarely dimmed by passing clouds. Strong winds descending from the Rockies tear across the prairie untamed by trees. The plains are harsh. Survival isn't cheap.

The plains zone and the alpine tundra, which lie thousands of feet apart in elevation, exhibit many of the same survival techniques. Plant species of the plains like western wheatgrass and June-grass are as short-lived as spring rains, bursting to life and flowering before the hot, dry winds of summer drive them back into dormancy. Far above the plains, and weeks later, alpine saxifrage competes with a short growing season by taking only five days to sprout new leaves, flower, and disperse pollen.

Speed is one survival technique common to both plains and peaks; patience is another. Blue grama grass is a model of patience, hoarding moisture by sending deep taproots into the plains soil, maturing slowly, and flowering later in the year during brief autumn rains. On the high peaks live even more patient plants like alpine phlox and moss campion, which may sprout only one or two tiny leaves a year and requires a decade to mature.

The surprising variety of such survival techniques in the Plains zone creates an intriguing ecosystem. Buffalo, antelope, and coyote depend upon the plains, as do long, dark strings of waterfowl which knit the orange skies of autumn. Colorado's state bird, the lark bunting, inhabits the plains. And, the Plains zone actually extends into the foothills of the mountains— sometimes as high as 5,500 feet—and so includes many species characteristic of Colorado's Foothills zone, where a mountain wonderland begins.

A Confluence

When two mountain rivers come together, the currents tangle and twist, boiling the water into waves. There is no pulse, no rhythm to the music of the waters. Such a confluence is like a symphony without a conductor. The clash of landscapes can be like that, too.

The Foothills zone in Colorado is a confluence of landscapes. It reflects as many other zones as it connects. South of the Palmer Divide which separates the Front Range from the Pikes Peak Massif, the low-lying hills covered with pinyon pine-juniper stands look greasy under a harsh sun. In the northeastern foothills of the Front Range and the Rampart Range, the zone is less distinct. On the western slope, the foothills of ranges like the West Elks are furred in a scraggly black winter coat of oak brush, a tangle of branches and trunks thick enough in places to tangle the wind.

The Foothills zone is a transitional zone that always seems to be under construction. At its lower edges, grassland and sagebrush species create the impression of confused prairie or shrub lands lost in the mountains. At its higher elevations, ponderosa pine and white fir spill down off the mountains along creeks. With little chance to develop a personality of its own, the Foothills zone resembles a border town. As such, it attracts the richest diversity of flora and fauna to inhabit any other life zone. And, like any border town, it showcases an interesting collection of characters.

From a distance, Gambel oak might be pretty, turning orange and red in autumn, casting shadows like charcoal etchings against the winter snow. But ranchers, hunters, hikers, riders, and anyone else who tries to travel through it find oak brush anything but pretty.

The branches of the Gambel oak look like an ingeniously designed trap. Sprouting from a single root system, an entire hillside of trees can share a single source, spreading out laterally to catch all the moisture trickling downhill. Packed close together, the branches swoop too low to crawl under and too high to crawl over.

To the Spanish who first moved across the West Elks and Uncompahgre Mountains, this land choked with oak brush was the chaparral, a term

For years there were more stories of moose in Colorado than there were moose. Scientific surveys concluded that decades of periodic sightings in the northern reaches of the state were of individual animals wandering into the state from Wyoming or Utah. Colorado had no viable or reproducing population of moose.

Then, in the winters of 1978 and 1979, a privately funded transplant program was conducted through the Colorado Division of Wildlife. Moose were brought in and released near the Never Summer Range and North Park. Today, Colorado's moose population has grown to an estimated 130 animals with more healthy calves added each spring. MICHAEL S. SAMPLE

derived from the Spanish word for evergreen oak. Leather coverings worn by riders for protection while breaking through brush like Gambel oak are still called "chaps."

But that same tangle of branches that halts hikers makes oak brush a valuable cover for wildlife such as rabbit, mule deer, and black bear and for birds such as green-tailed towhees and scrub jays. Long game trails honeycomb the deepest stands of oak brush like dark tunnels, cool in the day, sheltered from wind at night, and hidden from view at any angle. Wildlife feeds on the soft, nutritious acorns of Gambel oak or on serviceberry, the berries of kinnikinnick, or squawbush. The importance of this habitat as cover and as a food supply for wildlife has prompted the protection of foothills regions of the West Elks, the Elks, the San Juans, and other ranges under the National Wilderness Preservation System.

In south and southwestern areas of the state—in the foothills of the La Plata Range, San Miguel Mountains, Culebra Range, Spanish Peaks, and southern Sangre de Cristos—there is more space between trees. On these drier hillsides stand "pygmy forests" of pinyon pine and juniper, the forests of life for the Navajo, Utes, Pueblo, and other peoples of these mountain ranges. Pinyon wood was used for shelters, fence posts, furniture, and firewood. Sap from these small and gnarled trees was used to make glue, as waterproofing on woven baskets, and even as medicine in dressing wounds.

But pinyon nuts were the real life of pinyon forests. *Pinyon* is the Spanish word for nut. Every other year the cones of pinyon pines open and release tiny nuts which for centuries were collected by gathering tribes who worked their way up mountainsides, harvesting nuts and berries.

To collect these sweet and nutritional nuts, blankets were spread beneath trees and then branches were rocked or hit with long sticks to

Bristlecone pines are often twisted and gnarled into weird shapes by the wind, their almost indestructible wood polished into picturesque snags. Rarely exceeding forty feet in height, bristlecone pines often remain alive only in a narrow strip of weathered bark and a few needles. JACK OLSON

knock the nuts from cones.

In recent times, however, many acres of pinyon pines have been destroyed by "chaining," a technique using bulldozers to clear large tracts of land for grazing. The slow-growing pinyon pine-juniper forest, despite its rugged appearance, is actually quite delicate, and as many as three hundred years may pass after a major disturbance before the forest reaches its stable climax stage.

Still, the pinyon pine-juniper forest remains widespread throughout Colorado's southern and southwestern mountain ranges. Today, pinyon nuts are harvested with blankets as they were decades ago and sold at roadside stands as "Indian nuts" or "pine nuts." Today's traditional harvest recalls an ancient past, a time before old mountain ways collided with new days.

Music in the Pines

No silence is sweeter than that of a ponderosa pine forest in the mountain zone. There is no more musical breaking of that silence than the notes of a gust of wind through the branches. "Of all the Pines," said John Muir, "this one gives forth the finest music to the winds."

While ponderosa pines occur as low as 5,600 feet, the most magnificent groves in Colorado play their music between 8,000 feet and 9,500 feet, especially in the Front Range and San Juans. Although rare in northwestern ranges of the state, ponderosa is the dominant species of the Montane zone throughout the east slope of the

Rockies, inhabiting lower elevations farther north.

To sit in a mature ponderosa stand is to sit in a natural cathedral. The trees take 150 years to mature, finally standing more than a hundred feet tall and soaring fifty feet with little taper before the first branches appear. Long, lush needles filter the sunlight until it flows like honey on the forest floor, more shadow than light. In thin strands of sunlight, patterns of cinnamon-red bark look like the works of an artist in stained glass. The air, when the wind is still, smells faintly of vanilla.

Above all, in a ponderosa grove there is a feeling of space. Ponderosa pines need elbow room.

To capture enough water on dry, sunny slopes, the trees sink extensive root systems as deep as forty feet, with lateral roots spreading a hundred feet or more.

Between trees, the dim light that filters through branches cannot support a thick understory. Seedlings and brush which do manage a foothold—species like wax currant shrub, kinnikinnick, and ponderosa pine itself—are often killed by frequent ground fires ignited by lightning attracted to the tall spires of mature trees. Frequent small fires actually strengthen ponderosa stands. Thick bark protects mature trees from fires which cleanse the forest floor, reducing tinder which can trigger large crown fires. Small fires also return nutrients to the soil by breaking down thick litter accumulations, thus helping keep mature trees healthy.

Until recently, forest management techniques dictated the suppression of all fires, however small and beneficial. That practice left ponderosa pines susceptible to infestation by insects such as the mountain pine beetle.

The mountain pine beetle, a woodboring insect, is always present in low numbers in ponderosa pine forests. In healthy forests, trees expel the beetle from the bark by oozing pitch, and predators such as woodpeckers can keep the beetle population in check.

In forests weakened by short-sighted fire prevention, however, the mountain pine beetle population skyrockets as eggs laid in the bark of diseased trees hatch. Beetle larvae feed on host trees throughout the winter, weakening the forest further, then mature to fly off in search of new trees in the spring.

A stain of brown, dead trees can slowly spread through forests of ponderosa, killing thousands of acres. Mountainsides today in many parts of the Montane zone have lost the music of ponderosa pines.

There is other music in the Montane zone— bugles of elk as herds leave the high country in autumn; screeches of Stellar's jays; single-note chirps of chickadees; and long, metallic scoldings of pine squirrels. In sunny mountain meadows,

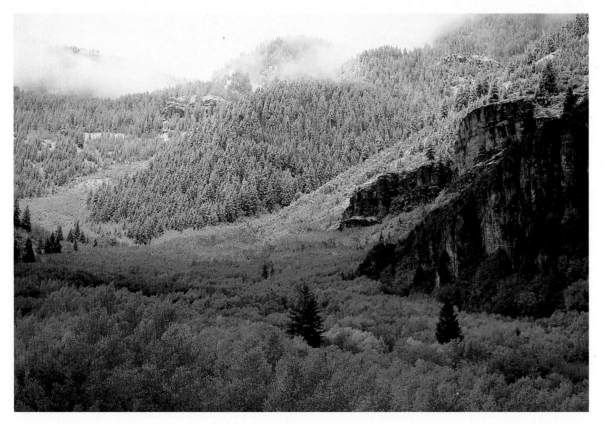

An early winter snow dusts San Isabel National Forest in the Sangre de Cristo Range—the same range which attracted Albert Ellingwood, one of the pioneers of Colorado mountain climbing, to "peaks unclimbed and peaks unclimbable."
TIM LUCAS

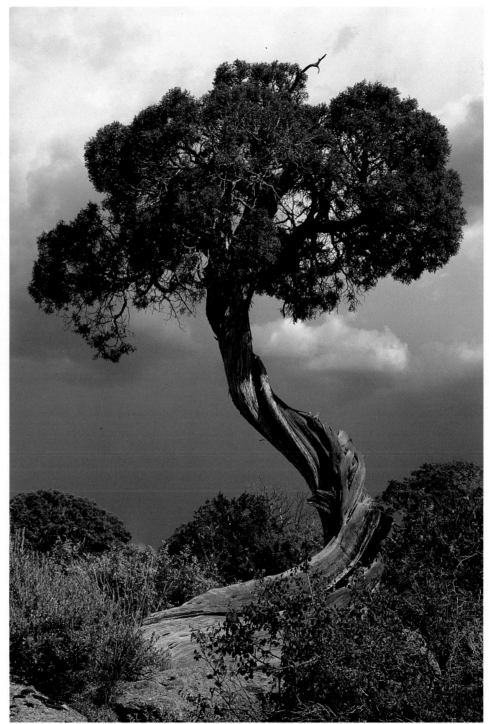

Howling winter winds, above, have piled this snowdrift in Rocky Mountain Park, while Hallett Peak and Flattop Mountain in the background are obscured by wind-blown snow. JOE ARNOLD, JR.

The stress of highcountry existence is vividly portrayed in the twists and swirls of this juniper, right, in the Black Canyon of the Gunnison National Monument. Windborne particles of sand and ice scour the bark off trees, contort branches, and stunt growth, but this persistent tree curls back and straightens toward the sun. LINDA WEEKS

monkshood and wallflower and larkspur add splashes of color to dark green ponderosa forests. On higher, damper, colder slopes of Colorado's eastern ranges, Douglas fir mixes with ponderosa while in the ranges west of the Continental Divide, Douglas fir is the predominant tree and ponderosa only rarely dots the landscape. White fir, too, joins the Montane forests in the south. And Colorado's state tree, the blue spruce, thrives along waterways and on the flanks of the state's northern ranges.

These forests differ from ponderosa stands. The dark Douglas fir forest permits even less sunlight to reach the floor. The air is cold. Shadows are as deep as the layers of needles which carpet the forest floor, hushing footsteps. The whooping of blue grouse echoes deep in the forest.

Unlike other Montane-zone conifers, white fir rarely dominates a mountainside, more often mixing quietly with other forests. The white fir is an impressive tree, with silver-gray needles and

cones that stand erect on branches like the candles of a traditional Christmas tree. And blue spruce lines streambanks far up into the mountains, coloring the creeks blue-gray at dawn.

The wind plays music in the sharp branches of blue spruce and hums in the long needles of white fir, too. But none of these species are as widespread or as domineering as the ponderosa pine. No forest has quite the magic or wonder or sacred feeling as the groves of ponderosa. It is ponderosa forests that remain in the memory long after the mountain days have passed.

A Season of Change

Ponderosa pine dominates Colorado's Montane zone, and the Subalpine zone just above consists chiefly of Douglas fir. But mountains never sleep. A spear of lightning ignites the tallest crown in a mature grove of ponderosa, setting off a forest fire. An avalanche roars down a mountain slope, snapping Douglas fir like matchsticks. Miners or

loggers leave behind shaved slopes. New seasons constantly begin in the mountains—seasons of change—and other species temporarily flourish.

In a raging winter storm, a patch of aspen becomes an apparition. Wind-blown snow cracks like knuckles in icy branches. Twisted shapes and fog-gray bark transform solid trees into swirling stormclouds. The whole grove seems poised to melt away into piles of finely crystaled snow.

Such impressions are not so far-fetched. In Colorado's mountains, neither aspen nor lodgepole pine are long-lived species, appearing and disappearing in little more than a human lifetime. Both are stages in a larger process. Both are signs of change.

Given an undisturbed environment, plant communities develop in a systematic pattern known as "succession," beginning with pioneer plants and evolving towards a stable, self-perpetuating balance called a "climax community." A climax community creates and maintains conditions favorable to its own species. For example, ponderosa pine saplings thrive in the shadowy sunlight filtered by mature ponderosas overhead. In the Montane and lower Subalpine zones of Colorado's mountains, ponderosa pine and Douglas fir are climax species, content to blanket every hillside if left undisturbed.

But the mountain never sleeps. If fire scorches the mountain landscape of northern Colorado, lodgepole pine invades the newly opened territory. When fire heats the cones of lodgepole pine to 113-122 degrees Fahrenheit, resin holding the cone scales tight melts and seeds are dropped. New lodgepole seedlings, which thrive in direct sunlight, quickly stubble the charred area.

If, however, there were no lodgepole pines in the area or the ground was cleared by something other than fire, aspen saplings will flourish. Increased sunlight after the climax trees have been destroyed heats the forest floor and stimulates the production of ''suckers,'' shoots of new aspen which sprout from the shallow web of aspen roots

Winter drives bighorn sheep lower, where this ewe, right, has found snow cover thin enough to paw through. Unprotected areas leave them vulnerable to predators and the whims of weather. But the greatest dangers have been suburban developments which destroy crucial wintering grounds and water projects which drown calving habitat. Bighorn numbers have dwindled and herds such as the one on Buffalo Peaks—once one of the largest in the West—have suffered greatly. MICHAEL S. SAMPLE

Colorado's state animal, the bighorn sheep, leads a life of contrasts. Below, under the warm summer sun, highcountry grasses provide lush forage and rugged cliffs and peaks protect the sheep from predators.
PERRY CONWAY/THE STOCK BROKER

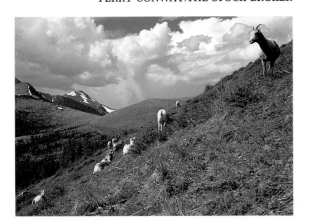

underlying broad areas of mountain country. Almost overnight, the ground goes fuzzy with aspen sprouts thriving, like lodgepole saplings, under the sun.

The entire process is amazingly swift in biologic terms. The invasion of new ground is completed and new groves established within just five to ten years. In fact, young aspen groves often reveal remnants of the climax forest—sawed stumps or charred wood left behind by the fire.

A lodgepole forest looks old from the moment it sprouts. Packed together like stick matches in a box, lodgepole pines grow so thick and straight that dead trees often have no room to fall and simply lean for years, giving the forest an unkempt look. A lodgepole forest is a quiet, empty place. Sunlight cannot penetrate through thick branches, and so the forest floor is practically a biological desert.

A young aspen forest, on the other hand, *looks*

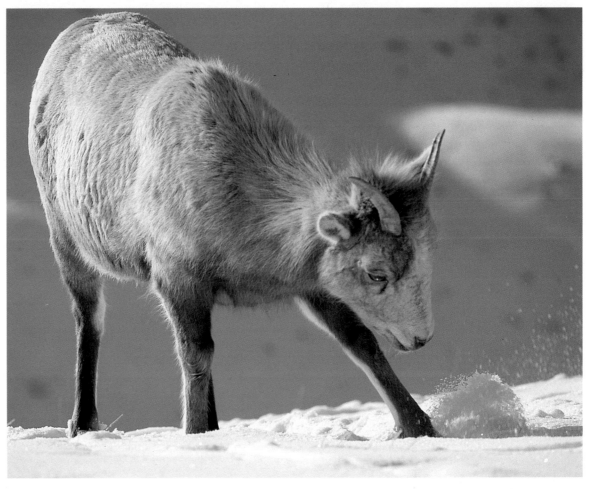

King of the mountain

Oreamnos americanus. *MICHAEL S. SAMPLE*

The mountain goat, *Oreamnos americanus,* is a newcomer to the Colorado Rockies, the new king of the mountain. A purely North American species, its haunts originally included the mountains of Canada, Alaska, Washington, Idaho, and Montana. Being a creature of the heights, the low dips in the Continental Divide of Wyoming proved an uncrossable boundary to the species and until May 24, 1948, the mountain goat did not appear in the Colorado Rockies.

On that day, on the flanks of Mount Shavano in the Sawatch Range, nine goats captured in Montana as part of a wildlife exchange program were released by the Colorado Division of Wildlife. It was only the beginning. Trading wild turkey, trout, bighorn sheep, and blue grouse, other mountain goats were secured from Idaho, South Dakota, and British Columbia. A total of fifty-one goats were released over a twenty-three-year period in places like the Collegiate Peaks, Mount Evans, the Gore Range, and the Needles.

The mountain goats thrived. By 1975, the population had reached 775 animals and was healthy enough for in-state relocation programs. Mountain goats now inhabit the West Elks, the Never Summer Range, and have been sighted in Rocky Mountain National Park and even atop Mount Sopris in the Elk Range.

new. Since each tree has sprouted from the same root system, it imitates the shape, size, branching pattern, even swirls in the bark of its neighbors. And the understory of an aspen forest is a garden. Displacement of the old, stagnant climax forest has thrown open competition for new niches. Purple pasqueflowers push up through lingering snowdrifts and the star-shaped flowers of blue columbine streak across meadows. Butter-colored sunflowers, white puffs of pearly everlastings, and sparks of Indian paintbrush and fireweed bloom wildly in the sunlight.

The sudden diversity of habitat in an aspen forest attracts wildlife, too, and each species leaves its mark on the trees. Yellow-bellied sapsuckers chip holes in the bark to trap insects or collect sweet sap. Wintering elk nibble at bark rich in Vitamin K, an essential vitamin for blood-clotting. (Cow elk, which use the quiet aspen groves for calving, may ingest the bark just before giving birth for this very reason.) Rutting mule deer, elk, and even moose re-introduced into the Never Summer Range use aspen trunks to rub the velvet off their antlers. Black bears rake the trunks with their claws, leaving long, striped wounds that blacken with age. Pointed, chiseled aspen stumps indicate the work of beaver.

Eventually life takes a heavy toll even on aspen, and a mature stand looks as gnarled and bent as arthritic hands. Within 25-50 years, groves of both aspen and lodgepole begin to die. Deep shadows thrown on the forest floor by the canopy of now-mature trees hinders seedlings. But that same shade, and the deep loam formed by years of fallen leaves, creates advantages for other saplings—Douglas fir or ponderosa pine, the same species swept aside to make room for the newcomers just one short lifetime ago.

Where the Wind Lives

Just as aspen and lodgepole pine give way to climax species, Colorado's Montane zone is replaced at higher altitudes by the Subalpine zone. Even on a still day, the wind is here, sculpted into the branches and bent-over forms of trees. This is the treeline. The wind lives here.

The forests of the Subalpine zone are the highest, snowiest, and windiest in the Rocky Mountains. At its lower reaches (at elevations around 10,000 feet), the lodgepole pines and Douglas firs of lower elevations blur its borders. The upper borders, however, are unmistakable. The Subalpine zone stops where the trees stop.

Timberline is not treeline. Timberline is the edge of tall upright timber. Treeline, less distinct, is the highest reach of trees in any form, twisted, bent, or broken. In Colorado, timberline is approximately 11,500 feet above sea level—higher on south-facing slopes, lower on north-facing slopes.

The Subalpine zone begins far below treeline. Two species dominate vegetation in this zone—subalpine fir and Engelmann spruce. Snowbanks linger far into summer. Dwindling populations of Canadian lynx and wolverine, both considered threatened species in Colorado, prefer the trees while herds of mule deer and elk forage in sunnier meadows through the summer.

As the Subalpine forest reaches the middle of its zone, it takes complete control. Occasional stands of aspen or lodgepole are short-lived in the cold and windy heights that favor spruce-fir forests. In fact, plant succession rarely occurs in the higher Subalpine zone. Disturbed environments above 10,000 feet are instead replaced in kind immediately, since no species from lower elevations can take hold in such harsh conditions.

More subtle than the flood of fall colors in trees at lower elevations, autumn on the tundra, above, nonetheless brings its own touches of beauty. Grasses turn brittle yellow while cushion plants turn red, orange, and brown.
KENT AND DONNA DANNEN

Even in an ecosystem as barren as a snowbank, life persists. Red snow, above, one of the strangest examples of nature's beauty, is caused by large numbers of a species of algae which has adapted itself to conditions in a snowbank. In summer, as small amounts of meltwater permeate a snowbank, the algae reproduce in numbers large enough to tinge the snow red. Where the algae is extremely prolific and the snow unusually red, the snow may even taste like watermelon. Climbers have reported footsteps turning blood-red behind them—an eerie phenomenon due to concentration of the red algae when snow is compressed. GARY SPRUNG/GNURPS PHOTOGRAPHY

Summer in the spruce-fir forest is pleasant if cool. Temperatures in even the warmest months average less than 50 degrees Fahrenheit, and the frost-free season is less than two months long. Yet the pale white flowers of Richardson's geranium and the heart-shaped, yellow flowers of the arnica both add color where the forest thins, and serve as food for elk and deer.

Winter, though, is different. The spruce-fir forest is empty. Deer and elk move to lower valleys where the snow is thinner. Pine grosbeaks descend to mixed forests to feed on buds. Only the tracks of an occasional snowshoe hare or even more occasional lynx break the snow. Only the wind breaks the silence.

Snow piles deep in the forest of the Subalpine zone, deeper by far than in any other mountain ecosystem. One storm on April 24 and 25 of 1921 dropped a national record of 76 inches of snow in 24 hours near Silver Lake in the Front Range. And snow not only falls from the sky—it also blows off the bare alpine tundra and collects in spruce-fir forests, packing deeply into shaded spots where it lingers long into July.

Neither snow nor cold, however, shapes this Subalpine landscape as powerfully as the wind does. Wind velocity increases with elevation, and at treeline blows nearly constantly, sometimes exceeding 100 miles an hour. Ice crystals driven like splinters of glass act as chisels to sculpt a strangely beautiful landscape known as the *krummholz,* a German word meaning "crooked wood."

The krummholz region officially begins at elevations where the average temperature of the warmest month equals 50 degrees. But no thermometer is required to recognize it. Branches of upright trees have been stripped away on the windward side. Buds facing the wind are nearly always killed, and those that survive curve back around the tree and trail downwind like streamers. These trees resemble unfurling flags and, appropriately, are called "banner trees."

Here even Englemann spruce and subalpine fir kneel down and crawl to survive, fleeing the prevailing winds in long, low mats pruned by the wind. Shoots on the windward side die, but shoots on the leeward side survive and so the plant rolls slowly downwind. At the Niwot Ridge Biosphere Reserve in the Indian Peaks, where much of the research on high-altitude life is conducted, wind-blown trees have slid far down the mountainside, covering old trails as if slowly making for the shelter of timberline. Winter snow shelters plants from the wind and insulates them from severe cold, but branches which stick out of the snow do not survive the winter. And snow which is too deep can shorten the already-short growing season.

This is, literally, life at the edge. The krummholz region is not a separate ecological zone, but rather a transition between Subalpine forests and Arctic-alpine tundra. This is where the wind lives, and those trees which come here must bow to the ground where it passes.

Tahosa

At first glance, the Arctic-alpine zone seems barren—as if the wind, no longer satisfied to simply subdue vegetation, has banished it altogether. No longer snagged in the branches of trees, wind slips over rock as easily as water flows over ice.

But the tundra is a place for more than first glances. It doesn't reveal itself easily. Only close inspection reveals the subtle threads that weave the tundra into a tapestry of life.

The tundra vividly displays a diversity of species. At the height of the short tundra summer, constellations of flowers sprinkle the landscape like stars in a mountain sky—sky pilot, rose crown, king's crown, stonecrop, and saxifrage. The droopy heads of old-man-of-the-mountain (''compass flower'') follow the sun across the sky. Elk string across ridgelines and bighorn sheep drift slow as summer cloudshadows, grazing.

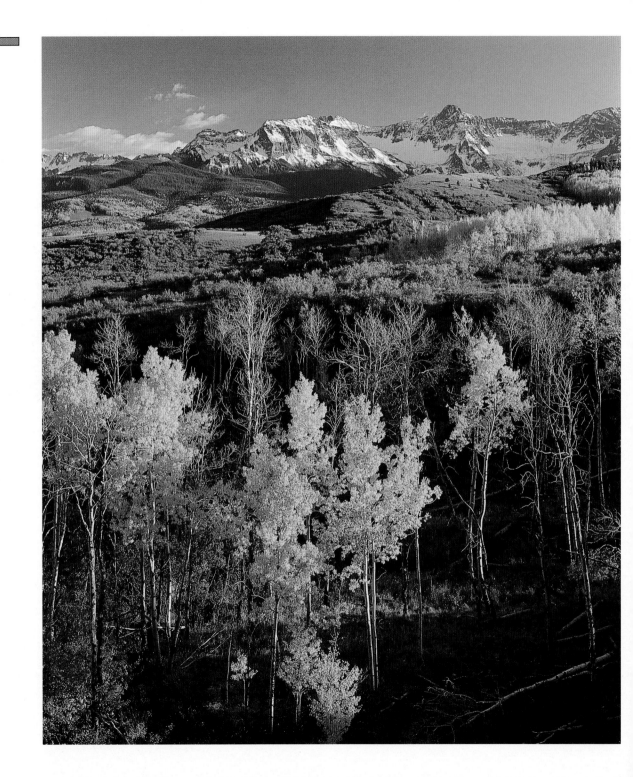

Swords from the sky

Autumn aspen at Dallas Divide, left, seem to ignite the Sneffels Range, one of several smaller ranges which make up the San Juans. The name of the Sneffels Range comes from the Nordic word for snowfield used in Jules Verne's classic book **Journey to the Center of the Earth.**
JAMES RANDKLEV

Lightning storm over the mountains.
LEO L. LARSON

The alpine tundra is the windiest of mountain zones. One wind gauge on Niwot Ridge in the Indian Peaks, maintained as part of ongoing studies by the Arctic and Alpine Research Station of the University of Colorado, shows that exposed ridge just south of the Continental Divide to be the third-windiest spot in the world. Only Fujiyama in Japan and Mount Washington in New Hampshire have recorded more wind.

Wind and snow determine the pattern in this tapestry. Pockets of snow, protected from the wind, provide enough winter warmth for less hardy species and promise water for more thirsty species next spring.

Much of the wind-blown tundra is snowless. On windward slopes, where soil is stripped to bare rock, no snow offers insulation or replacement of moisture sucked away by winds. These are fellfields, often called "alpine deserts." Life clings even here.

Cushion plants, species like moss pink and alpine phlox, survive by hugging the ground and closing in on themselves like fists. They grow no taller than a few inches. They grow so slowly— one, perhaps two, tiny leaves sprout each brief growing season— that decades pass before they flower and a plant the size of a handprint could be 150 years old. They form furry cushions which act as sponges, trapping moisture, particles of wind-blown soil, and warm air. Temperatures within the tiny mats of this tundra quilt can be twenty degrees Fahrenheit warmer than surrounding air.

The thin leaves of sedge kobresia, or elk sedge,

A few years ago, a helicopter carrying Division of Wildlife personnel circled slowly over a barren plateau high in the Colorado mountains, trying to believe what they saw below. There on the tundra lay a herd of sixteen elk, all dead. Later, scientists theorized that the elk had been grazing close together when a storm gathered quickly, catching them in the open. A bolt of lightning smashed into the ground nearby, killing all the elk instantly.

Tornadoes seem more violent and floods get more publicity, but according to the National Weather Service, lightning is responsible for more weather-related deaths in the United States than any other element. It is sharp and quick as a sword from the sky, killing more than a hundred people a year in the United States.

The mountains of Colorado, sticking their rocky summits into the sky, are lightning rods in a storm. Between 1978 and 1983, fifteen people were killed by lightning in Colorado, most of them in the mountains. Yet, by following a few simple rules, the hazard can be drastically reduced.

Most thunderstorms in Colorado occur in late afternoon, after clouds have built lazily all day.

You can reduce your risk of lightning strikes by climbing early in order to reach a summit by noon, and by leaving a mountain and remaining below timberline during storm hours. If caught by a sudden storm in the mountains, avoid exposed ridges and summits. Find a low spot part way down the mountain, but do not lie flat. Lying flat exposes a large surface area of the body to current flowing through the ground. For the same reason, leaning against a cliff face is dangerous. Groups, if caught in exposed areas, should scatter to lessen the odds of lightning hitting the entire group.

If a strike does occur, first aid should begin on the victims immediately. A lightning victim does not retain any electrical charge from a lightning bolt, which can carry up to 30,000 amperes of power. Artificial respiration and cardiopulmonary resuscitation may be necessary as well as treatment for burns from the heat of more than 30,000 degrees Celsius which can result from a lightning bolt.

Mountain storms can be beautiful and inspiring—a few precautions and some simple common sense can keep that beauty from turning into a nightmare.

are a signal of soil. Pockets of roots and humus form slowly, requiring hundreds of years to get just a foot deep. But that is deep enough to anchor the most diverse community on the tundra—alpine clover, sky pilot, gentians, white-crowned sparrows, horned larks, and an array of lichens. When the short summer is in full swing and every species blooms, these are the most colorful designs in the tundra tapestry.

Elsewhere on the tundra, the depth and duration of snowdrifts, not soils, determines which species survive. Where thin snowbanks melt quickly, Parry's clover and willow shrubs as tall as fingers appear. Snow buttercups impatiently push through deeper, lingering drifts. Flowers, grasses, and sedges emerge from the last melting snow so late that the petals of alpine avens are already tinted with sunset colors and elk sedge has turned gold, heralding the alpine autumn.

Even higher, where mountains stop and sky begins, only lichens can scrape life from the rock. Lichen is a symbiotic life form, a partnership between fungus and algae. Fungus provides a latticework which anchors the plant, while algae produces food through photosynthesis. Green, orange, red, and black lichens, resembling

Tiny lakes called "tarns" like this one in Montezuma Basin dot Colorado's highcountry, formed by meltwater in depressions cut by retreating glaciers. Many tarns are only a few inches deep and remain frozen far into summer, supporting scant life but adding delicate touches to mountain scenery. SPENCER SWANGER/ TOM STACK AND ASSOCIATES

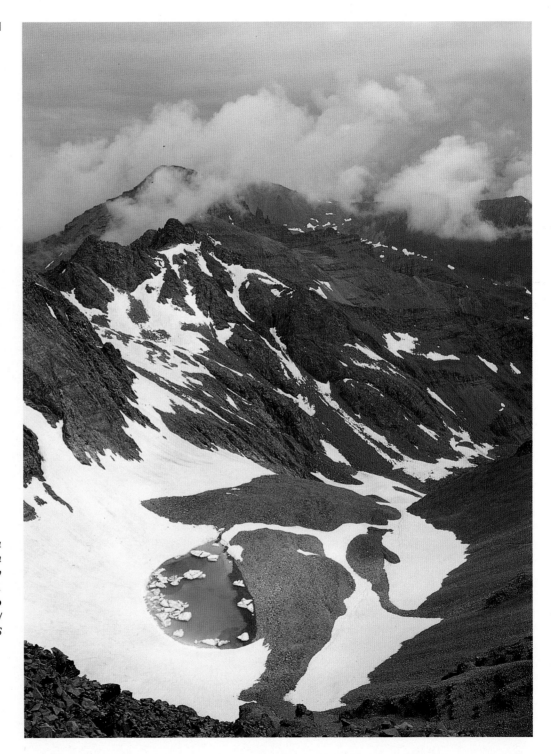

splotches dripped from a paint can, survive on scant nutrients found on the granite itself, slowly breaking solid rock into tiny fragments of soil, paving the way for other species.

Above the lichens, there is only sky. *Tahosa,* the Kiowa Indians called these sacred summits, ''the top of the mountains.'' Views unfold like a hand in greeting. In valleys, creeks shine like strands of silver among wildflowers. Dark green Douglas fir, gray-blue Colorado blue spruce, the silver bark of aspen—to look down from such heights, from the crest of the world, is to survey the earth from atop a rainbow. ■

Delicate columbine emerges from between granite boulders in the Mosquito Range. Much of the Mosquito Range is within Pike National Forest, yet only the Buffalo Peaks section in the southern part of the range is being considered for protection as a wilderness area. DAVID MUENCH

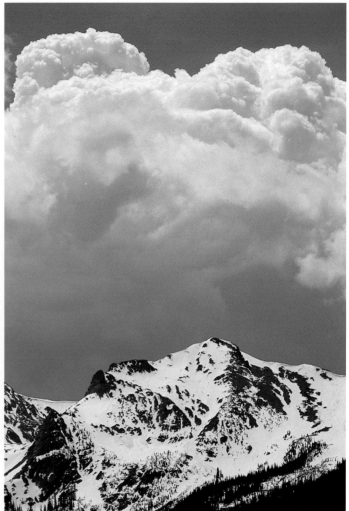

Cameron Pass, above, at the north end of the Never Summer Range is often the scene of dramatic weather shifts. Strong mountain winds funneled through the pass and boiling air masses over the surrounding peaks can transform sunny skies into a raging storm within minutes. JACK OLSON

Winter's first snow has blanketed this ranch below Mt. Hayden, left, in the Sneffels Range of the San Juans. Some of the heaviest snowfall levels in the West are recorded in the San Juans, and several major rivers—the Piedra, La Plata, San Juan, Rio Grande, and Cimarron—have their headwaters in the range. DAVID MUENCH

Left, the earth and stars seem to revolve around this isolated cross-country ski hut in Colorado's Rockies. DAVID HISER

A rotary snowplow, above, undertakes the enormous task of opening Trail Ridge Road in Rocky Mountain National Park. More than a million visitors travel Trail Ridge Road each year, despite the fact that tight curves and deep snow keep this highest paved road in any national park closed all winter. JOE ARNOLD JR.

Aspens

Aspen such as these in the San Juans, left, are transitional or pioneer trees, the first to revegetate an area disturbed by avalanche, fire, logging, or other disturbance. Direct sunlight favors aspen shoots and the trees grow quickly. A new grove may mature within a decade. But aspen, by creating shade, favor young coniferous trees which eventually will replace the aspen. LARRY ULRICH

Perfectly still water mirrors this stately grove of aspen near Ilium Valley, below. GEORGE POST

Aspen often sprout from underground tubers after disturbances and provide prime wildlife habitat and conditions suitable for many species of grasses and flowers. With the first touch of autumn, aspen leaves turn gold and carpet the forest floor, returning nutrients to the soil, right. JEFF GNASS

The slender white trunks of these aspen contrast with the dark mass of Gothic Mountain in the Elk Range, far right. DENNIS W. JOHNS

Mountain wildflowers

One of the many advantages of Colorado's varied topography is that spring comes to the Rockies in waves of magnificent color, advancing up the mountainsides with summer. Flowers of the plains bloom while the mountains are still mantled with snow. Then when the plains are dry and brown, the highcountry is just beginning its magnificent wildflower display.

Few places in the world rival the ecological diversity of Colorado's mountains, where an estimated three hundred species of wildflowers grow.

The shooting star, top left, is named for its flaring shape. MICHAEL S. SAMPLE

Food for bears and early mountain inhabitants, the glacier lily, middle left, is one of the first flowers to signal spring. MICHAEL S. SAMPLE

Alpine phlox, bottom left, grows above timberline, withstanding the ravages of mountain wind. MICHAEL S. SAMPLE

Summer flowers, below, drench this meadow in the La Plata Mountains with color. DAVID MUENCH

Dwarf clover and alpine forget-me-nots mingle in Rocky Mountain National Park. JEFF FOOTT

Colorado blue columbine blooms in Yankee Boy Basin of the San Juans, left. Columbine, the state flower, belongs to the buttercup family and is found in moist, cool aspen groves and open meadows. *DAVID MUENCH*

The red columbine, above, is one of several species of flowers related to the Colorado blue columbine. *DOUG LEE*

"Old Man of the Mountain," the alpine sunflower, below, takes years to send down a sturdy taproot before flowering once and then dying. *JOE ARNOLD JR.*

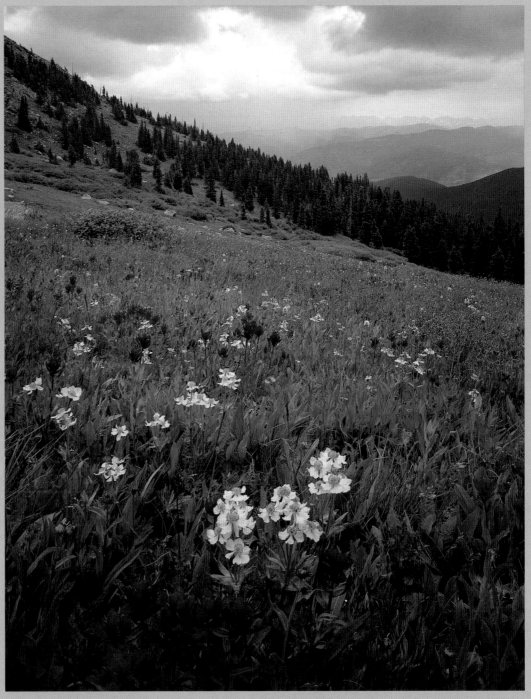

Calypso orchids or fairy slippers, above, grow in secluded areas such as Wild Basin in Rocky Mountain National Park in moist ground and dim light. R.C. DOHRMANN

Familiar to most mountain travelers, red Indian paintbrush and cloud-white marsh marigolds, right, are among the most beautiful and abundant mountain wildflowers. These adorn a hillside in the Holy Cross Wilderness of the Sawatch Range. JEFF GNASS

Mountain wildlife

Bighorn sheep, right, is Colorado's state animal.
MICHAEL S. SAMPLE.

The swallowtail butterfly, top left, is one of a wide variety of colorful insects found in Colorado's mountains. MICHAEL S. SAMPLE

A female mountain lion and her cub, bottom left, peer down from a ledge in Boulder County. A solitary animal, the mountain lion— also known as cougar, puma, or panther—is abundant but rarely seen in the Colorado mountains. PERRY CONWAY

Mule deer, above, are the most common large mammal in the Colorado Rockies, found in all of the state's habitats from grasslands to tundra. MICHAEL S. SAMPLE

With its slow metabolism and effective defense, the porcupine, top left, is content to slowly chew away at the bark, twigs, and leaves of trees. Although seemingly slow, one porcupine can do extensive damage to a grove of trees. MICHAEL S. SAMPLE

Like marmots, pikas, such as this one atop Mt. Evans, left center, send out sharp alarm calls at the approach of hikers. But the pika, unlike the rodent marmot, belongs to the rabbit family and does not hibernate. JEFF MARCH NATURE PHOTOGRAPHY

More than any other animal, the beaver, bottom left, first brought white men to the mountains. Valued for its pelt, the beaver was almost trapped into extinction in the Rockies until rescued by a whim of fashion which made beaver hats less popular. Today, the beaver population is increasing in Colorado. GREGORY K. SCOTT

When quiet autumn mornings are pierced by the eerie bugling of bull elk in rut, battles are frequent. Using their massive antlers, top left, the bulls compete for the right to mate with cows. *MICHAEL S. SAMPLE*

Found along clear streams from prairie to mountain top, the water ouzel or dipper, bottom left, is specially adapted for feeding in the cold water, where it hunts aquatic insects by walking on the streambed or swimming underwater by using its wings. *MICHAEL S. SAMPLE*

The white-tailed ptarmigan, bottom right, is a mottled brown during much of the year. But in winter the ptarmigan turns pure white and, feeding on willow buds near timberline, spends all year in the snowy highcountry, almost invisible. *MICHAEL S. SAMPLE*

Their whistles are so familiar to hikers and climbers that yellow-bellied marmots, right, have become known as "whistle pigs." Marmots live in rock slides and talus slopes, browsing on vegetation, sunning themselves, and hibernating in the winter. *WENDY SHATTIL/ROBERT ROZINSKI*

The shape of the sky

The mountains of Colorado give shape to the sky.

Backlit by the sun of morning, every range has its own skyline. The long, flat back of the Rampart Range, the broken-glass edge of the Sangre de Cristos, the slow rolling Mosquito Range, the silent bells of the Elks, the spires of the Needle Range, all carve their own angles into the Colorado skyline.

Spotlit by the sun of evening, every peak has its own profile— the perfect symmetry of Lone Cone in the San Miguel Range, the spire of Lone Eagle Peak in the Indian Peaks, the rounded summits of the two Buffalo Peaks in the Mosquito Range, the double wedge of Arrow and Vestal peaks in the Grenadiers, the caricatures of Lizard Head and Rabbit Ears.

Sometimes, the names speak for themselves— Squaretop, Flattop, Jagged Mountain, Pyramid Peak, and Notch Mountain. The names of other peaks are more poetic—Sharkstooth, Wolf Tooth, Keyboard of the Winds, Wham Ridge, the Three Apostles, and the Zodiac Spires. Still other peaks are given only numbers for names (Peak Twelve in the Needles Range), or letters (Peak C in the Gore Range), or are given no name at all.

As long as humans have left footprints among Colorado's peaks, as long as humans have named Colorado's peaks, humans have wondered how mountains were formed and why they look like they do. To the southern Ute Indians, mountains like Pikes Peak were formed when the Great Spirit spun a stone into a mountain, breathing on snow to form creeks and shaking trees so that falling leaves became birds.

To the Utes, peaks like Sleeping Ute Mountain sprang up where one member of their tribe, who were once giants, guarded the camp while the others hunted. The hunters were gone for centuries and the lone Ute finally lay down to rest, slowly turning to stone.

Other ancient peoples wondered, too, and told of Upsacanda, a giant warrior who stood as tall as a man on horseback and could uproot trees with his hands. One day, Upsacanda fell into a bottomless hole and got lost underground. The swells and bumps of the mountains are his poundings from below as he searches for the single way out.

Geology is the newest legend. Like legends of old, geologic theories—or more particularly geomorphology, the science of landscape—change a bit each time they are told. New information is verified, other information discredited. New techniques, new ways of thinking constantly add clues. Every crack in a cliff face, each swirl in summit rocks embellishes the story of how the Rocky Mountains shaped Colorado's skies.

In an ancient shadow

Mountains are not new to Colorado. Neither are swamps, seas, or deserts. Each has, in turn, danced across the Colorado landscape.

Globally, evidence of geologic history dates as far back as 4.4 billion years. In Colorado, however, the oldest rock records found to date come from the 2.3 billion-year-old Uinta mountains

A rainstorm over the Tenmile Range, left, helps in the slow sculpting of Colorado's landscape.
DANN COFFEY/THE STOCK BROKER

The ruins of an ancient mountain range, the Ancestral Rockies, are evident at Garden of the Gods below Pikes Peak, right. MICHAEL S. SAMPLE

in the northwest corner of the state. Details of the Colorado landscape during this time—the Precambrian Age—are as dark as the Precambrian rocks which today cap some of the state's highest summits. What ancient clues *can* be read show an endless battle between uplift—the force that raises mountains—and erosion, which tears them down.

At least three times during the Precambrian Age, mountains were raised in Colorado, and following each episode of mountain building the earth rested and erosion wore those mountains down into low hills, even level plains. Mountains, in fact, are as fleeting as snow drifts in geologic terms. Were it not for new uplifts, erosion would sand the globe as flat as a cue ball in 25 million years.

As the Precambrian Age ended 570 million years ago, Colorado's mountains had endured a long erosional period called the "Lipalian Interval." Advancing seas of the next great geologic epoch, the Paleozoic Age, swept back and forth across the flattened landscape and the highest summits in the state were those of wind-swept waves.

These seas did not actually build mountains, but they did deposit the bones of modern Colorado ranges. Sediments settled to the sea floor and formed the Sawatch Sandstone found today on many peaks in the Sawatch Range. Paleozoic sediments are also common on the east slope of the Mosquito Range, in the heart of the Sangre de Cristos, and around ranges such as the Wet Mountains, the Gore Range, and the Park Range. Fossils from these ancient seas are exposed in both the Sawatch and Mosquito ranges.

About 300 million years ago, in what geologists call Pennsylvanian or late-Paleozoic time, the quiet Colorado landscape began to rumble and rise again. Periods of uplift known collectively as the Colorado Orogeny continued for millions of years, eventually thrusting two major mountain ranges from the sea. The most easterly of these mountain islands—"Frontrangia"—was a huge range extending from the Wyoming border far into southern Colorado and following a course just thirty-five to fifty miles west of the present Front Range from which it takes its name.

The second ancient range was just as large, beginning south of the Colorado-New Mexico line, swinging along the western edge of the present-day San Luis Valley and past the Black Canyon of the Gunnison, Colorado National Monument, and the present course of the Colorado River. Taking its name from the Uncompahgre Plateau in western Colorado, this ancient range of mountains is known as "Uncompahgria." Summits like Pikes Peak and Mount

Since the last volcanic ash of eruptions in the La Garita Mountains settled to earth, erosion has been carving a masterpiece in the Wheeler Geologic Area, left. Wind and rain slowly melted volcanic tuff and ash-formed rocks into fluted walls, rounded knolls, spires, and pinnacles. Formations like "The City of Gnomes," "Phantom Ships," and "The White-Shrouded Ghosts" are secluded deep in a roadless section of Rio Grande National Forest. These formations were designated a national monument in the early part of this century, but that designation was rescinded because of the area's inaccessibility. Today, however, the Wheeler Geologic Area is being considered for protection as part of the National Wilderness Preservation System. F.J. BAKER

Evans already stood over these Ancestral Rocky Mountains, but no one knows what other modern peaks and ridges carved the Colorado sunsets.

Once these Ancestral Rockies were born, the earth rested again, as if wearied by mountain-building. Erosion clawed deep. By the end of the Pennsylvania Period, around 270 million years ago, crumbling mountains had filled the surrounding valleys with deep sediments that hardened into new rock, adding more bones to the skeleton of modern Colorado mountains.

The Fountain Formation, a red-tinged sandstone sloughed from Frontrangia, is visible at the Flatirons of Boulder, in the Garden of the Gods near Pikes Peak, and at Red Rocks Park near Morrison. Another of the sediments washed off Frontrangia, the Minturn Formation, makes up the bulk of the Sangre de Cristo Range and parts of the Sawatch Range.

Uncompahgria left its legacy of erosion as well. Sediments from the summits of this ancient range, carried down the slopes by snowmelt and wind, rose again in the Maroon Formation which today includes perhaps the most beautiful peaks in the world—the Maroon Bells of the Elk Range.

The third great division of time, the Mesozoic Age, brought to Colorado lapping seas, windy deserts, and swamps tracked with dinosaur footprints. Before new ranges cast their shadows across the Colorado landscape, 160 million years slipped by. The earth slept, resting, preparing for the birth of a new mountain system.

A new thunder

About 65 million years ago, during a period known as the Laramide Orogeny, the earth began rumbling once again, lifting the greatest mountain chain in the world—the modern Rocky Mountains, which reach their greatest width, more than three hundred miles, in the heart of Colorado and Utah. The Laramide Orogeny was part of a worldwide mountain-building episode resulting in such great mountain ranges as the Andes in South America, the Alps in Switzerland, and the world's highest peaks, the Himalayas in Asia.

The Laramide Orogeny slowly and persistently uplifted the Rocky Mountains for 20 million years. Then erosion gained the upper hand, as it had with the Ancestral Rockies, raking streams deep into newly raised sediments, redepositing them layer by layer in valleys until the peaks themselves stood hip-deep in boulder fields, islands in a sea of sediment.

Had that erosional cycle continued, the Rockies would have been leveled. But another period of mountain-raising, the Miocene-Pliocene Uplift, raised Colorado and its neighboring states by 5,000 feet. It was this uplift, which rocked the

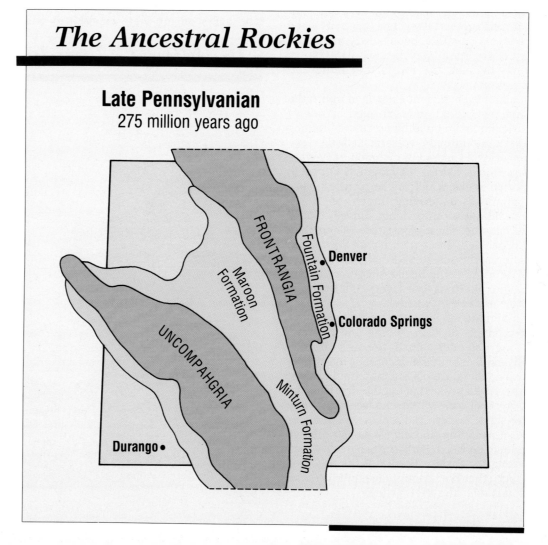

The Ancestral Rockies

Late Pennsylvanian
275 million years ago

FRONTRANGIA

Maroon Formation

Fountain Formation

Denver

Colorado Springs

UNCOMPAHGRIA

Minturn Formation

Durango

earth from 28 million to 5 million years ago, which made modern Colorado the highest state in the nation. Once the Miocene-Pliocene Uplift ended, Colorado again cast a formidable shadow.

A mountain born

Imagine a force so patiently persistent that in the course of millions of years it can raise a level plain into a mountain range an inch at a time. Imagine a force so powerfully gentle that in its wake the rock layers, or strata, bend slowly to hug the contours of the mountain like wind instead of shattering. Imagine the forces that built Colorado's mountains.

Throughout each ancient episode of uplift, the mountains of Colorado were formed by one of three basic mountain-building processes—folding and faulting, doming, or volcanic action.

The majority of Colorado's mountain ranges are faulted anticlines. During the Laramide Orogeny, Precambrian rocks which make up the "basement complex" underlying much of North America shattered into long, linear blocks beneath Colorado. These blocks rose. Where they bent and buckled softer rock layers above into sleek patterns, they created formations known as folds. Where the rising blocks shattered overlying rock into sharp, jagged layers, the resulting formations are known as faults.

Most mountain ranges in the southern Rockies are the products of such folding and faulting. Their long, slender, north-to-south trends, especially evident on relief or contour maps, give them away. These are classic mountain ranges, with knife-edged peaks that cut the sky. Faulting of thick layers of rock, where one face rises while the other sinks, has created ranges which tower over the surrounding landscape—the Park Range looking down on North Park, the Sangre de Cristo Range along the eastern border of the San Luis Valley, and the Wet Mountains building like stormclouds over the Wet Valley.

Where folding and faulting occur together, the combination can be artistic. Ranges take on asymmetric shapes. The Tenmile and the Mosquito ranges, both folded to the east, roll gently upwards to the abrupt edges of large faults which have axed the steep cliffs of their western slopes.

The high ranges pushed up by folding and faulting have black eyes. As their dark, Precambrian cores rose, the soft, light-colored sedimentary layers on top were exposed to wind and water erosion and stripped away. The summits of ranges like the Mummy Range, the Rawahs, and almost all faulted anticline mountains in Colorado are composed of dark schists, granite, and gneiss—the basement rocks. The one notable exception is the crest of the Sangre de Cristo Range, one of the youngest faulted anticlines in the state, so young that the sedimentary layers still cap its summits.

The supreme faulted anticline in Colorado is the

Building Colorado's mountains

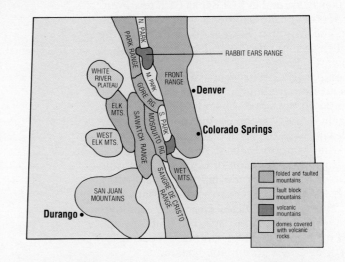

A powerful quartet: *Four distinct and powerful geologic processes gave rise to Colorado's immense mountains, and each is visible today.*

folded and faulted mountains
fault block mountains
volcanic mountains
domes covered with volcanic rocks

Folds: *When two segments of the earth's crust collide the surface may buckle or fold. Larger folds may override and bury smaller ones.*

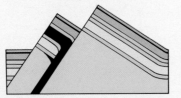

Faults: *Underground pressure breaks rock along lines of weakness. Vertical faults result when land masses rise or sink. Horizontal faults result when land masses shift sideways.*

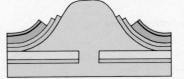

Domes: *Molten rock pools in underground pockets of the earth's crust, bulging the ground above as it cools. Erosion bares the hardened rock as a round or oval-shaped mountain.*

Volcanoes: *An eruption of lava and cinders from deep within the earth can create volcanic cones. Lava may also flow out along rifts in the earth's surface.*

Front Range. Like the blade of a broadaxe, the Front Range slices a ridge from the Wyoming border south to Canon City, the longest continuous uplift in the state. The steep fault along its eastern front, rising like a roadblock to the eastern plains, and the corresponding fault on the west show that the Precambrian rock was displaced as much as 15,000-25,000 feet. The peaks of the Front Range never stood that far above the sea; constant erosion prevented that. But the geologically sudden rise left chips of rock like shards of shattered glass at places like the Flatirons in Boulder. The core rock tore through sedimentary layers like a slow-moving bullet, and the Flatirons are the tattered edges of the bullet hole.

Pools of stone

Unlike the great surges of the earth's crust which take place during folding and faulting, the doming process involves no movement of core rocks. A domed mountain is cast like iron.

Molten rock, often granitic, collects in pools or bubbles beneath the upper layers of rock strata, prevented from sinking deeper by hard, impenetrable layers below. This hot bubble of liquid rock beneath the earth's surface slowly cools, hardens, and expands to be known as a "batholith" if it stretches more than forty square miles. As it expands, it blisters layers of rock above, arching them upwards.

During periods of general uplift, the hardened bubble rises toward the surface. Erosion, meanwhile, chews away at the overlying, exposed mounds of soft rock. Eventually the dome is exposed. A mountain is born.

The Colorado landscape is dotted with such peaks cast in batholiths. The most famous is Pikes Peak. The pink granite dome of Pikes Peak formed from molten rock more than a billion years ago, which means it stood as a recognizable peak of the Ancestral Rockies. The Pikes Peak batholith dominates the geology of the lower

Front Range. The Rampart Range, seen from the east as a long, flat-topped ridge north of Pikes Peak, is also underlain with Pikes Peak granite. Both the Tarryall and Kenosha mountains are underlain by a batholith.

Farther north in the Front Range, Mount Evans, the peak which overlooks Denver, was born of a huge flow of molten rock 1.7 billion years ago. The slow-cooled rock of Mount Evans, coarse-grained and filled with minerals, was, like Pikes Peak, pushed up as part of the Ancestral Rockies and then again as a part of the modern Rocky Mountains.

Smaller, lens-shaped intrusions of molten rock formed in much the same way as batholiths are "laccoliths." Peaks like Mount Crested Butte, which rises 2,000 feet above the town of the same name in the Elk Range, and Hahns Peak in the Park Range are both laccoliths.

Batholiths, laccoliths, dikes such as those that radiate from the Spanish Peaks like the spokes of a wheel—all of these are the once-molten by-products of another, deeper fire that surfaced elsewhere and changed the face of Colorado's mountains.

Fire on the mountain

The Spanish Peaks almost smell like smoke, and the morning stars over Rabbit Ears Peak look like sparks. These peaks were forged as the legacy of volcanic activity which at least three times sparked the skies of Colorado.

Although no active volcanoes remain within the modern Colorado Rockies, the Rocky Mountains belong to the Pacific Belt, which includes active peaks in the Aleutian Islands, the Andes of South America, the Cascades of Mount St. Helens fame, and a string of other hot ranges where 80 percent of the world's active volcanoes are located.

Scattered hot spots once smoldered throughout Colorado—the White River Plateau, the Never Summer Range, the Rabbit Ears, Buffalo Peaks

in the southern Mosquito Range, the Spanish Peaks in the southeast, the West Elks. But the real center of activity, the furnace door, was the San Juan Mountains, and the landscape cast by these volcanoes is awesome.

The San Juans are a kingdom, 10,000 square miles of peaks comprising the largest single range in the United States Rockies. The San Juans could hide whole eastern states within their shadow. The range contains thirteen peaks over 14,000 feet and scores more over 11,000 feet. At the center of many lies a heart of fire.

The Laramide Orogeny had already begun pushing other ranges up when the San Juans were born. In fact, a huge dome a hundred miles across slowly rose in the San Juan country during the early part of that uplift, but later eroded again, exposing the hard shell of Precambrian rock.

Then 35 million years ago, sparks started to fly. Volcanoes in the southern and northeastern part of the range erupted in chorus, spewing lava, dust, rock, and flame over hundreds of miles and burying the landscape nearly a mile deep in volcanic debris. Again and again, for 5 million years, lava flows swept down valleys and joined in rivers of fire that spread across what is now the San Juan country and the West Elk Range.

Then, the volcanoes quieted. But before erosion could finish its clean-up job, volcanoes near Silverton erupted in an encore performance, creating a new lava flow forty miles across and a half-mile high.

The next quiet phase lasted longer. A million years of silence in the San Juans was not interrupted until, 29 million years ago, violent eruptions occurred around Treasure Mountain. Volcanoes as broad as sixty-five miles shook the range with such force that at least fifteen peaks collapsed in on themselves in calderas which can still be identified. The eruptions ceased in only 2.5 million years, but the show was not over.

As the Miocene-Pliocene Uplift raised the San

Towards two shores

The backbone of the continent, the Continental Divide, winds through Colorado from the northern Park Range to the southern San Juans. The Divide separates streams which flow west into the Pacific Ocean from those which flow east into the Gulf of Mexico and the Atlantic Ocean, but it follows few of the highest peaks in the state.
TRANSPARENCIES UNLIMITED

A storm gathers over the mountains of the Continental Divide, clouds as dark as wet rocks sagging with water. The air above the peaks smells like rain, which suddenly comes in sheets, obscuring ridges. Although the raindrops fall on the same peaks, they will flow down different rivers to oceans thousands of miles apart.

The Continental Divide runs 1,700 miles through the United States from Montana to New Mexico. On the flats of Wyoming and in New Mexico deserts, it is little more than a gentle swell of the landscape. But in Colorado, the legend of the Continental Divide comes alive.

From the north, the Divide enters Colorado on the back of the Park Range, running south until it first crosses a major road at Rabbit Ears

Pass. Then it swings east along the Rabbit Ears Range toward the Never Summer Range and Rocky Mountain National Park, where millions of visitors annually encounter the Divide at Milner Pass on Trail Ridge Road.

As the Divide swings south to the Indian Peaks, following summits as jagged as broken glass, it takes on its legendary grandeur as the "ridgepole of the continent," as Will Rogers called it. Then at Sawtooth Mountain, the Divide reaches its easternmost point in North America.

Continuing south along the Front Range, the Divide reaches its highest points—Grays and Torreys peaks, the only two of Colorado's fifty-four 14,000-foot summits that are in its path.

Crossing west between the Mosquito and Tenmile ranges, it continues south along the Sawatch Range and towards the "big bend" in the San Juans, where it swings as far west as the Needles and then bends towards Wolf Creek Pass before leaving the state for New Mexico.

It is a powerful feeling, standing on the Continental Divide and watching a rainstorm gather above, feeling raindrops drip off one hand on their way to the Pacific Ocean while those off the other hand begin the long journey to the Gulf of Mexico and the Atlantic Ocean. And on the Divide, where the continent splits apart, travelers—like raindrops—must continue their journey towards one of two shores.

Juans and the Rockies to the sky, a final major burst of volcanic activity 25 million years ago coated the eastern San Juans in black basalt. A few more eruptions in the San Luis Valley to the east of the San Juans were only echoes of that greater volcanic thunder. Silence, which has lasted until today, returned to the San Juan Mountains.

Of a sculptor's touch

The graceful lines of folding, the jagged cliffs of faulting, the bubbles of batholiths and domes, the firebrand peaks of volcanic activity—these are the processes which, during geologic upheavals like the Laramide Orogeny, built the Colorado Rockies. But mountain-building is only half the story. The Colorado landscape, after the long thunder of uplift quieted and the sparks of volcanoes cooled, would have been only vaguely recognizable today. The peaks and ranges were unfinished, raw as a painter's half-empty canvas. The crowning touches would not be added by forces which raise mountains, but by those which tear them down.

The hills at the southern end of the Mosquito Range roll like ocean swells on the horizon of South Park. Summits are low; gradients slope easily. These are quiet peaks and once much of the Colorado Rockies looked like this.

From atop the last swells of the Mosquito Range, though, the view west over the Arkansas Valley encompasses the jagged heart of the Collegiate Peaks in the Sawatch Range. Here, the terrain is broken, rough-cut, and chiseled. The landscape has been shattered into spectacular cliffs and ridges.

Similarly, dark, wooded mountains east of Estes Park roll like a green carpet toward the plains. Yet west of Estes Park, sharp peaks in Rocky Mountain National Park tatter the horizon.

Pikes Peak owes much of its fame to the fact that it is the easternmost of Colorado's tallest peaks and thus was a landmark for early pioneers. It also boasts a greater base-to-peak relief than any other Colorado peak—approximately 6,600 feet. MICHAEL S. SAMPLE

The difference between such ranges, a difference within a few miles, is staggering—and caused by ice. Almost every sharp cliff and pointed spire in the Colorado Rockies owes its dramatic profile to ice.

The story of ice begins innocently enough, one snowflake at a time gathering during the deep winters of Pleistocene time. The uplifting of mountains had stopped. Volcanoes had subsided, but clouds of smoke and ash still dimmed the sun. The snows were deep nearly 3 million years ago, the cold was sharp, and both stayed long. Short summers fought a losing battle against snowdrifts, which became permanent slivers of winter, the first strokes of a tool which, more than any other,

chiseled the modern face of the Rocky Mountains: the glacier.

Before glaciers, much of Colorado's landscape was unspectacular, resembling the southern Mosquito Range where glaciers never existed. When the glaciers retreated, however, they left in their wakes the sculpted forms of today's breathtaking skyline. Before glaciers, the Rockies were uncut diamonds; afterwards, wherever glaciers had existed, the Rockies were jewels.

Pleistocene winter swept down from the polar reaches in huge caps of glacial ice which covered as much as 5 million square miles of North America, from northern Canada deep into Missouri and southern Illinois. In the west, a

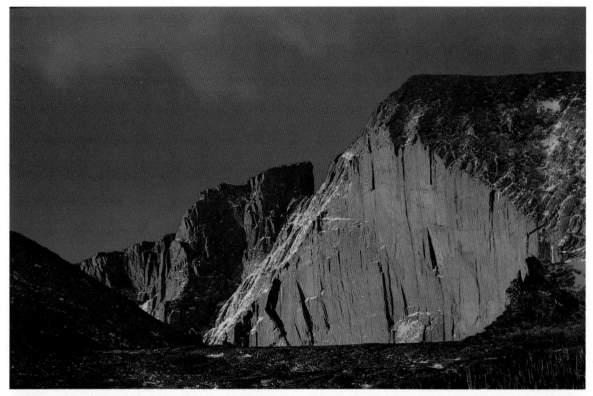

gigantic lobe of ice 1,200 miles long and 400 miles across engulfed the Canadian Rockies and dipped into the mountains of northern Montana, Idaho, and Washington.

These ice sheets advanced and retreated for thousands of years in at least four major glacial periods. In none of their advances did ice sheets reach the mountains of Colorado.

Although Colorado was not in the path of the great ice sheets which Louis Agassiz, a nineteenth-century geologist, called "God's great plough," the snowflakes of Pleistocene winters gathered in cracks and crevices of the state's high peaks, slowly forming hundreds of smaller "valley glaciers."

One-third of the Rocky Mountain Chain above 6,000 feet was, at one time or another, covered with glacial ice. In the Colorado Rockies, nearly every mountain range—from the Park Range to the La Plata Range and from the Front Range to the Needles—bears the scars of glacial action as far down as 8,000 feet and some, like the San

Juans, even lower. Valley glaciers sharpened peaks into spires, gouged valleys, sheared mountains like Half Mountain in Rocky Mountain National Park in two, cut ridges, and sliced cliffs.

Snowflakes falling on a quiet evening are perfectly six-pointed. Lying loose in a new drift, fluffy and light, these points form air pockets between snowflakes. But as more snow piles on top year after year, and as upper layers undergo alternate periods of melting and refreezing, the brittle points of snowflakes break off. The snow packs tighter, into pellet-like crystals of ice called "neve," the seeds of a glacier.

These seeds, under great pressure, meld into deep, heavy slabs of pure ice groaning under their own tremendous weight. When an icefield reaches a critical density and weight, it slowly, almost imperceptibly, begins to flow downhill. Sculpting begins.

Glaciers carve two kinds of landscape: in one, surface material is excavated, while in the other, debris is deposited. One process carves mountains

and valleys; the other dams lakes and lines mountainsides with "moraines," piles of excavated debris left behind when a glacier retreats.

When mountains are excavated by glaciers, ice itself scours the rocks. That ice also uses dislodged debris to scrape the landscape. The sides and bottom of a glacier, then, although they move more slowly than the heart, are literally the glacier's cutting edge.

As hundreds of valley glaciers formed high in Colorado's mountain ranges, meltwater slowly seeped into tiny cracks, refreezing to form long, icy claws sunk deep into mountainsides. As those glaciers moved downhill, the claws plucked great slabs of rock from the mountains, leaving steep, three-walled gouges called "cirques."

Cirques are the most obvious chisel marks of glaciers, and there are thousands of them in Colorado. Mountains like the Sangre de Cristo, Sawatch, Gore and Park ranges are peppered with cirques and dotted with the tiny, sky-blue lakes called "tarns" which formed in cirques when glaciers melted.

The Bottomless Pit on the flanks of Pikes Peak is the remnant of a glacial cirque 1,700 feet deep. Horseshoe Mountain near Fairplay was gutted by a large glacier, leaving behind a cirque that gives the mountain its name. Perhaps the most famous glacial cirque, however, sits at the east face of Longs Peak in Rocky Mountain National Park. Here, an ancient blade of ice called the Roaring Fork Glacier chewed its way into the heart of the peak, leaving behind the 2,000-foot sheer drop known as "The Diamond" which challenges rock climbers and still serves as a landmark visible far out on the eastern plains.

When glaciers eat their way towards the heart of a peak from more than one side, they sharpen the summit like a hand-chipped spearhead, digging long sloping troughs out of mountainsides and leaving razor-thin ridges called "aretes" separating the cirques. Every climber worth his weight in hardware knows the challenges of ridges like the Ellingwood Arete on the northeast side of the Crestone Needle in the Sangre de Cristo Mountains.

In addition to cirques and aretes, the spiked summit left when glacial ice melts out of such cirques is known as a "horn," the classic mountain profile. Spires formed this way abound in Colorado—the Wetterhorn and the Matterhorn in the San Juans; Lone Eagle Peak on the western edge of the Indian Peaks, carved by the double-edged sword of Peck Glacier and Fair Glacier; and the ice-carved symmetry of Lone Cone in the San Miguel Range. Almost every sharp ridge, every pointed spire in Colorado's Rockies owes its existence to an artist, and that artist was ice.

Crashes and crevasses

Not every glacier in Colorado, however, melted thousands of years ago.

In 1844, William Hallett was hiking across a large snowfield in what would later become Rocky Mountain National Park. Suddenly, he was swallowed by a gaping "crevasse," a crack two feet wide, thirty feet deep, of an unknown length, lined with ice, and not supposed to be there.

True glaciers were not known to exist so far south in the Colorado Rockies. But stuck in the frozen crack, Hallett realized that such a crevasse could occur only in a glacier, not in a mere snowfield. If he ever got out of the crack alive, thought Hallett, news of such a find would cause quite a stir in the geologic community. He did, and it did.

Around 7,000 years ago, Colorado's climate started growing warmer and drier. Glaciers which had fought the sun to a stand-off at about 8,000 feet began to retreat quickly. Winter did stage one brief comeback about 800 years ago, in what has been called the Neoglaciation Age, or "Little Ice Age," but for the most part the claws of glaciers were retracted, exposing the artwork of peaks, U-shaped valleys, waterfalls, and high-country cirques. Only tiny slivers of ice remained, artifacts of once-great icefields.

The majority of these glacial remnants are strung like cold pearls along the Continental Divide as it follows the Front Range, especially in Rocky Mountain National Park and its contiguous wilderness area to the south, the Indian Peaks. The high peaks of the Front Range form an enormous drift-fence, capturing wind-blown snow in deep-pocketed cirques where the same processes which created huge glaciers in the past continue.

Today's glaciers are generally stable and quiet. Arapaho Glacier, tucked up tightly against the Divide between North and South Arapaho Peaks in the Indian Peaks, is the largest remaining glacier in Colorado. It stretches from 13,300 feet high in an east-facing cirque to 12,075 feet. The air-clear water flowing off the glacier supplies water for the city of Boulder.

Since Arapaho Glacier is part of a municipal water supply, much of it is off-limits to the public. The largest glacier most hikers can explore is Andrews Glacier to the north in Rocky Mountain National Park. As large and white as it seems today, as cool as the breezes are which blow across it even in mid-summer, Andrews Glacier is little more than a chip of the huge Bartholf Glacier which once filled many valleys in this part of the Front Range. Sprague, Tyndall, Rowe, Taylor, and Mills glaciers remain within Rocky Mountain National Park, St. Vrain and Isabelle glaciers within the Indian Peaks. St. Mary's Glacier, near the Fall River, attracts thousands of tourists each year.

In addition to glaciers, permanent snowfields like those on Mount Zirkel dot the Park and Mummy ranges. Snowfields pattern the high peaks like patchwork quilts in almost every major Colorado range. Even "rock glaciers"—talus slopes where ice and frost have lubricated loose rock, which slowly grinds its way downhill— still polish the Elk Mountains, the Sangres, and other ranges.

Now, though, these tiny remnants are chiefly oddities, tourist attractions reminiscent of massive rivers of ice flowing a thousand feet thick, like the glacier which carved Tenmile Gorge at the southern edge of the Gore Range. Visitors come to ski in July and imagine winter that never turned to spring.

In one effort to publicize a Colorado glacier and attract tourists, Fred Fair and the Denver & Interurban Railway offered a one thousand dollar prize in 1923 to any stunt pilot who would land a plane on the icy runway of the St. Vrain Glacier. The prize went unchallenged until a young barnstormer landed in Boulder, boasting that he would land anywhere for a thousand dollars. Fair, after seeing that the plane was virtually held together with baling wire and bubble gum, rescinded the offer on the grounds that the pilot would never be able to take off again. The pilot, however, assured Fair that he had no intention of taking off again. The prize, he argued, was for "landing" the plane, after which he would simply leave it there. Still, a crashed plane and an injured or dead pilot were not the kind of publicity Fair and the Denver & Interurban Railway wanted, so they withdrew the offer.

The barnstorming pilot flew off, without landing on the glacier and without the thousand dollars. The story might have ended there, except that four years later, in May of 1927, that same young pilot landed his plane, "The Spirit of St. Louis," in a cornfield outside of Paris to become the first person in history to fly solo non-stop across the Atlantic Ocean.

Today, not far south of the St. Vrain Glacier in

Colorado's mountains: Nature's ice sculptures

Anatomy of a glacier

The crack, or bergschrund, *at the head of a glacier occurs when ice pulls away from snow clinging to the mountain. Movement of the glacier scrapes out a steep hollow, or* cirque, *below the crack. After the glacier melts, the cirque may hold a lake or tarn.*

Farther downslope, crevasses *form as the ice moves over uneven ground. These cracks may be as narrow as a couple of inches or as wide as 40 feet and as deep as 120 feet.*

Chunks of rock break off along fractures to form a glacial staircase. *Rock debris, picked up by the bottom or sides of a glacier, helps ice grind its way down the valley. When the glacier melts and retreats, excavated debris is deposited along the sides and at the toe of the glacier in piles called* moraines—*jumbles of boulders, gravel, and earth.*

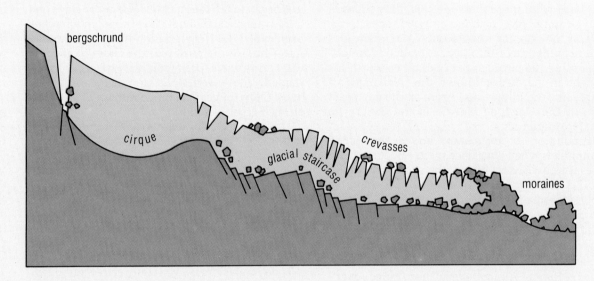

Carving valleys with rivers of ice

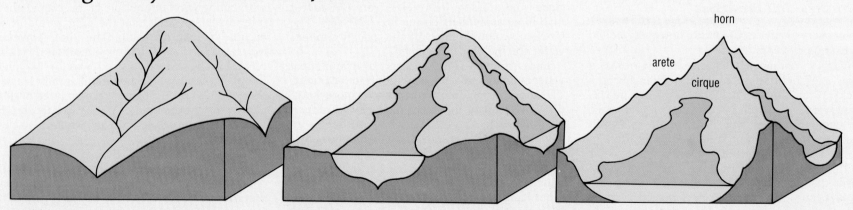

Before glaciation: *In steep terrain, fast-moving water cuts V-shaped valleys into weather-rounded mountains and meanders to avoid obstacles.*

Glaciation: *Ice and snow form glaciers at the heads of stream valleys. As those glaciers flow downhill, they deepen and straighten the valleys, scouring valley walls to form smooth-sided, U-shaped glacial valleys.*

After glaciation: *Once glaciers melt, the valleys they gouged are exposed. Glaciers descending in several directions from some summits carve pyramidal peaks called horns and sawtooth ridges called aretes.*

the Indian Peaks Wilderness, Lone Eagle Peak, according to a Denver Post reporter, "points a solitary finger skyward." The peak's name honors the man who wanted to land on St. Vrain Glacier, one of the greatest aviators in history—Charles Lindbergh, the "Lone Eagle" himself.

Publicity stunts, the flickers of flashbulbs from tourists' cameras, and an occasional ice climber or summertime skier provide most of the glacial activity in Colorado today. Yet some evidence indicates that the Rockies are still rising, slowly, and that we may also be living in a kind of glacial "Indian summer," awaiting the return of perpetual cold and its icy claws. Colorado's mountain scenery, the grandest on earth, already bears the unmistakable signature of an ancient artist, but that artist—whose time is endless and whose tool is ice—has not finished yet. ∎

Colorado's mineral belt

Colorado's mineral belt, a fifty-mile-wide swath of riches, joined the Cripple Creek mines to the east in yielding nearly $1.5 billion of gold, silver, copper, lead, and zinc by 1920, barely sixty years after the first gold strike at Cherry Creek. Since the 1920s, however, alloy minerals such as molybdenum, vanadium, and tungsten have become increasingly significant. In 1980, molybdenum production topped 102 million pounds, accounting for 83 percent of all metallic production in Colorado. Vanadium and tungsten, account for only a fraction of mineral production, but are important domestic sources of strategic alloys.

Primary Minerals

gold
silver
lead
zinc
iron
tin
copper
tungsten
molybdenum
vanadium

BOULDER
Nederland
GILPIN
EAGLE
Empire
Georgetown
Golden
SUMMIT
CLEAR CREEK
JEFFERSON
Breckenridge
Climax
PITKIN
Leadville
LAKE
Fairplay
PARK
CHAFFEE
TELLER
Tincup
GUNNISON
Cripple Creek
FREMONT
OURAY
Ouray
Silver Cliff
Telluride
CUSTER
Silverton
Creede
SAN JUAN
MINERAL
HINSDALE
LA PLATA
Durango
Denver

Having fun in the mountains

The mountains provide a measure of our strength, spirit, and skill. For centuries, since the first peak was climbed, Colorado's mountains have beckoned us to challenges and rewards. A skier feels the pull of the mountain in wind ripping past; a climber feels the strength of rock; a camper or angler feels the peace of solitude. Hiking, photography, sight-seeing, camping, and dozens more outdoor activities in the mountains attract most of the 12 million out-of-state visitors who spend $2 billion every year in Colorado.

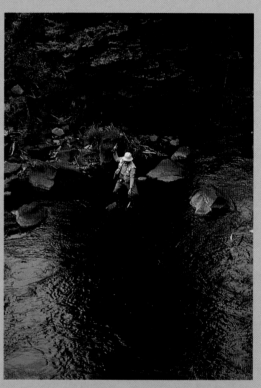

More than 750,000 people a year, including this angler, above, near Steamboat Springs, purchase a Colorado fishing license and try their luck in the state's mountain streams. KEITH KNIGHT

Snow plus sun equals winter fun in Colorado's mountains. Skiing in Colorado has become big business—in 1985, Colorado's 32 ski areas recorded more than 9 million visitors, left. BRUCE BENEDICT/ THE STOCK BROKER

Hiking near Capitol Peak, left, is not as easy as it looks. The Hayden Survey Party reported the Elk Range was a "region in which the rocks have been thrown into a greater state of chaos than we have ever observed anywhere in the West." STEPHEN TRIMBLE

Some mountain activities, like photographing subalpine wildflowers in Rocky Mountain National Park, rely on subtler challenges, top right. KENT AND DONNA DANNEN.

The rivers of Colorado swell with spring run-off and with wave after wave of whitewater boaters such as this Arkansas River kayaker in Seidel's Hole, Brown's Canyon, bottom right. DOUG LEE

With the freedom of the winds, a hang glider, above, rides the air over Bear Creek Canyon near Telluride. *KEN GALLARD*

For centuries, people have explored wildernesses on horseback, and pack train trips like this one in the Weminuche Wilderness, top left, are still a popular method of backcountry travel. *TOM BEAN*

This camper at Williams Lake in the Weminuche Wilderness, bottom left, has the world to herself. *TOM BEAN*

A new layer of powder brought these skiers together at Steamboat, top right, where they wait in lift lines to join 9 million other skiers tracking the snow of Colorado slopes. *NICHOLAS DEVORE III/ASPEN*

Backcountry travel—shown here near Independence Pass, bottom right—offers solitude, beauty, and good snow. *TIM LUCAS*

A climber ''lays back'' in a crack in the ''Athlete's Feat'' route on Castle Rock, Boulder Canyon. *JOE ARNOLD JR.*

Echoes among the peaks

Today, the first silent clues to human life in Colorado's mountains are lined in neat rows behind the glass of museum cases. Projectile points 11,000 years old, found in the Indian Peaks, are light to the touch—and cold. Sharpened by rock against rock, some still hold an edge and could slice flesh even now. Spearheads taken from the flanks of Longs Peak date back 9,000 years.

Early man came to Colorado from the north, moving across the Bering Land Bridge from Asia 10,000-30,000 years ago, moving quickly south in search of land unlocked from glacial ice. The high country was still frozen, so the first signs of life are found low—in the San Luis Valley below the Sangre de Cristos, and at the "Lindenmeier Site" in the northern Front Range. Then the ice began to melt, timberline rose rapidly, and the high country teemed with life. For the first time, human voices echoed among Colorado's peaks.

Colorado's mountains meant meat for hunters. For gatherers, the hillsides meant blueberries, kinnikinnick, currants, wintergreen, and pinyon nuts. Early inhabitants gathered herbs like marsh marigold and fireweed and alpine sorrel, dug the roots of yampa and alpine spring beauty, crushed the flowers of yarrow. The mountains meant survival—and more.

One mountain in the northern Front Range is rather small as Colorado's mountains go. At first glance, it does not inspire the awe that other peaks do. But Old Man Mountain was special. People from many different tribes climbed to its summit, alone, bearing gifts and seeking visions. Here, the sacredness of the four directions—north, south, east, and west—unfolded and life became clear, ordered, like light through a prism.

Strange relics collected on the summit of Sitting Man Mountain: a river-worn rock weighing twenty-five pounds and rounded by water into a near-perfect sphere; slivers of glass-clear obsidian valued and rare in the area; exquisitely crafted and delicately patterned artifacts. What visions were revealed for these offerings there is no way to know—only that the early people of the mountains came here, sat in stillness for days, and then climbed back down, leaving behind strange gifts.

The summit of Longs Peak once contained an oval depression deep enough to conceal a crouching hunter. An Arapaho Indian brought back to the Estes Park area in 1914 by the Colorado Mountain Club said the structure was the eagle trap of "Old Man Gun" who, in the early 1800s, often lay at the summit with the carcass of a coyote nearby, waiting for eagles. When an eagle landed, Old Man Gun grabbed it by the talons, quieting the fierce bird with a balm rubbed on his hands and stomach. Feathers from the eagle, used in a ceremonial headdress, supposedly gave the wearer great power.

Blanca Peak, the southern prow of the Sangre de Cristo Range, towers over the San Luis Valley. The first recorded climb to its summit, in 1874 by members of the Wheeler Survey, revealed a "circular depression possibly used by Indians as a shelter for their sentinels." The structure may have been instead a hunting blind for bighorn sheep, an eagle trap like Old Man Gun's, or a religious shrine. No one knows. The Indians who built it are gone and the rocks are silent.

Because they were nomadic people, following herds and weather, these mountain people left behind no elaborate cities of stone like the Indians of Mesa Verde did. Because the rock of mountains is granitic and hard to work, they left few pictographs or petroglyphs like the rock art of Fremont Indians in western canyons. And because of the harsh climate, few of the more fragile and perishable artifacts of their lives have survived to the present.

Still, in the Front Range alone forty-two stone game drive systems have been identified. More than 26,000 prehistoric sites have been identified in the state. The feet of countless generations wore trails across places like Ute Pass into South Park and Cochetopa Pass, called the "Buffalo Gate," leading to the huge buffalo and elk herds of the San Luis Valley. Sightseers today who drive Trail Ridge Road in Rocky Mountain National Park actually follow the ancient "Dog Trail" over the mountains into the hunting grounds of Middle Park. Modern travelers, like Indians before them, cross the Rabbit Ears Range over Willow Creek Pass to enter North Park, what the Indians knew as the "Bull Pen" for its vast elk and buffalo herds.

These are scant clues from which to reconstruct innumerable generations of mountain life. Man's shadow has fallen among the peaks of the Colorado Rockies for at least 10,000 years. The first mountain people hunted bighorn and buffalo, elk and deer; they gathered plants in the valleys; they died. The rest is guesswork, conjecture. Although archaeologists continue to search the mountains for clues, those early mountain people seem to have come and gone, leaving only the faintest of echoes among mountain peaks.

The eyes of a nation

Pike and Long are two names synonymous with Colorado mountains. Yet, neither Zebulon Pike nor Stephen Long ever set foot on the peaks which now bear their names. Lieutenant Zebulon Pike attempted a climb of Pikes Peak on his 1806 expedition but, equipped with only light cotton summer uniforms in spite of the fact that it was

Crested Butte Mountain, right, and the rest of the Elk Range have a geologic history as colorful as their pioneer and mining histories. Intense subterranean heat and pressure transformed old sandstones and shales which once comprised the ancient Uncompahgria Range of the Ancestral Rockies into the colorful quartzites and slates which were later uplifted to form the Elk Range.
DENNIS W. JOHNS

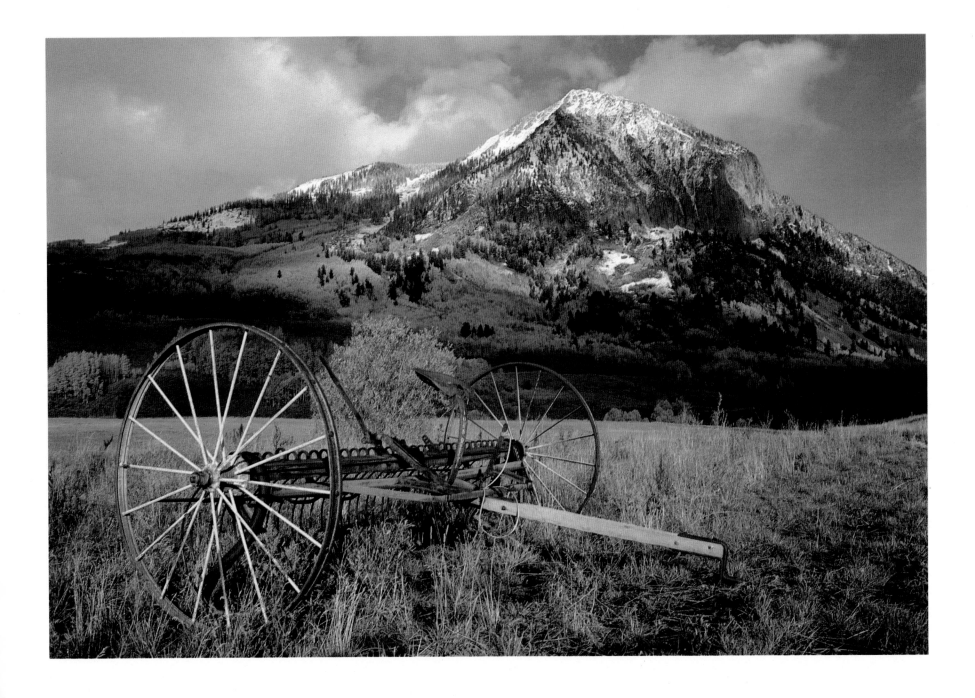

November, "no stockings," and no concept of the scale of the western landscape, he and a small party of men bowed to the mountain still "15 or 16 miles from us, and as high again as what we have ascended" and backed down. Standing in snow and with the temperature hovering below freezing, Pike declared that "no man could have ascended to its pinacle."

Because the peak bears his name, his brush with what he called the "Highest Peak" is Pike's most celebrated contribution to Colorado mountain history. But after leaving Pikes Peak unclimbed, he turned north to explore parts of the Rampart Range and the southern Mosquito Range. From the northernmost point of his travels he saw the highest peak in Colorado, Mount Elbert, and the second-highest, Mount Massive, both in the Sawatch Range.

Despite seeing all three, Pike remained convinced that Pikes Peak was higher. He wrote in his journal that the "height of this mountain from the level of the prairie was 10,581 feet, and admitting that the prairie was 8,000 feet from the level of the sea, it would make the elevation of the peak 18,581 feet." He was wrong, of course. Pikes Peak stands at 14,110 feet, Mount Elbert at 14,433 feet, and Mount Massive at 14,421 feet. Still, Pike was the first official to see all three.

Turning south from the Sawatch Range, Pike and his party circled back along the Arkansas River, confused and lost in this huge landscape, eventually crossing the Wet Mountains and then the Sangre de Cristos via Medano Pass. Blaze marks on trees leading to the pass showed prior use by the Indians. By this time, Pike's party had cut up their blankets for stockings, and the hip-deep snow they were hiking through atop the pass convinced Pike to·call the range the "White Mountains."

Atop the pass, Pike gazed out and saw "by lengthy vista at a distance, another chain of mountains." He thus became the first government official to survey the awesome breadth and grandeur of the San Juan Mountains.

Although his papers were seized by the Spanish when Pike mistakenly erected a fort beyond the American border, he later rewrote his journals from memory. Their 1810 publication marked the

Forever and longer

Twisted and stunted, their trunks rubbed the color of worn silver by centuries of wind-driven slivers of sand and ice, the ancient bristlecone pines on the Walter Pesman Trail in the Mount Goliath Natural Area are a testament to both the ruggedness of alpine habitat and the tenacity of life.

From Berthoud Pass south, growing on ledges where their roots grip cracks in the rock like claws, these pines are the oldest living things in Colorado, reaching 1,500-2,000 years. Growing at altitudes from 7,000 feet to treeline, the bristlecone is a solitary species, taking root in places where other species cannot survive. The cold in winter, the heat in summer, and the wind constantly batter the trees until their branches look like old bones hiding only a thin thread of living bark. Yet the bristlecones live on with a patience like rock.

One tree, called Methuselah, in the White Mountains of California, has been dated at more than 4,600 years old, making it one of the oldest living things on earth.

Just over Colorado's Cochetopa Pass on August 31, 1853, the first scientific specimen of bristlecone pine, a single branch, was collected by F. Creutzfeld of the Gunnison Expedition. That branch was later identified and classified by John Torrey and Asa Gray, two eminent botanists whose names rest on a pair of famous Colorado peaks. It was also in Colorado that the bristlecone pine received its first protection with the 1932 designation of the Mount Goliath Natural Area.

The bristlecone pine grows slowly, shedding its dark green needles once every three decades instead of in two- to three-year cycles like other pines. Its wood is infused with a resin keeping it rot-resistant and hard as iron. Today, scientists are studying growth rings from fallen bristlecone pines as if they were ancient calendars, looking for clues to long-term climatic patterns, perhaps even an indication of man's impact on the world environment. The bristlecone pine, after all, has been watching for centuries.

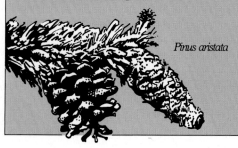

Pinus aristata

first official English-language account of the West and its peaks. His words introduced the fledgling nation to Colorado's mountains.

Unlike Pike, Major Stephen H. Long, leader of the 1820 government expedition to the Rockies, never even tried to climb his namesake. In fact, he and his men skirted much of the Front Range, coming no closer than forty miles to Longs Peak and mistaking it for "the point designated by Pike as the highest peak." Whether or not Long's party knew which peak they were looking at, they were close enough for Samuel Seymour, the expedition's artist, to sketch the view from what is now the town of Fort Morgan, thus presenting the world with its first visual account of the Rocky Mountains.

Later, standing on a minor summit in the Rampart Range, Long and the others saw the real Pikes Peak. For three of the party, including Edwin James, a climb to the summit was irresistible.

Edwin James was the talented 23-year-old botanist, geologist, surgeon, and journal-keeper of the Long Expedition. He had translated the Bible into Ojibwa to bring Christianity to the Indians and, on July 13, 1820, he and two others left the "boiling springs" at Manitou for the first recorded climb of a major Rocky Mountain peak by white men.

James was accompanied by a wagonmaster named Zachariah Wilson and a rifleman named Verplank, carrying a weapon against possible Indian attack. A French guide led them to the base of the mountain and then turned back, assuring them the peak was unclimbable because of deep sand and gravel on its flanks.

The party climbed until dark, still well below timberline, and passed a fitful night. Early the next day, they cooked breakfast, stashed the extra gear except for "three pounds of bison flesh," and launched their summit assault expecting to return to the same camp by nightfall.

Once the team broke treeline, they stood where

Home was where the ore was, or as close to it as possible. Log cabins, saloons, stores, and even an occasional church sprang up wherever miners struck paydirt, including Silver Lake in the San Juans. LARRY ULRICH

no scientists had stood before. James' botanical interest in the unusual species of plants and flowers he found there slowed the party down, but it also made him the first botanist in North America to observe and collect specimens of alpine tundra vegetation.

By 4 p.m. on July 14, 1820, the three men stood atop the summit of Pikes Peak, the first such group to scale any major U.S. peak and record their feat in writing. But James was more a scientist than poet, and his journal passage contains no rhapsody, only comments on the topography, weather, a swarm of grasshoppers, animal tracks, and the smoke of a distant Indian encampment. Less than an hour after reaching the summit, they began the descent.

Darkness fell before they reached their base camp. The trio spent the night in a hastily constructed camp without blankets while the temperature dropped to 38 degrees. In the morning, having "few comforts to leave," the party set out at first light and almost immediately noticed a plume of smoke in the direction of their base camp. After ruling out Indians, they discovered that the fire "raging over several acres" had been sparked by their campfire of two nights before and had ruined much of their gear. Gathering up "a beggarly breakfast" from the coals, they quickly made their way back to the main party.

In honor of the climb, Major Long suggested the peak be named for James, but the idea did not take hold. It is still Pikes Peak and Longs Peak

To walk among the mountains

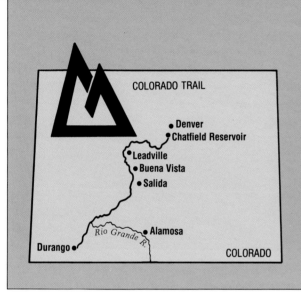

COLORADO TRAIL

• Denver
• Chatfield Reservoir
• Leadville
• Buena Vista
• Salida

Rio Grande R. • Alamosa
Durango •

COLORADO

Trails are nothing new to the mountains. Pike, Fremont, Hayden, and even the early miners followed well-worn Indian paths over major mountain passes and into river valleys. But the 480-mile Colorado Trail, which was completed in 1987, is different. In one continuous ribbon, it connects many of the major mountain ranges in the state, stretching from the Front Range near Denver to Durango in the San Juan Mountains.

Its route was planned with scenery, wildlife habitat, ecosystems, historical sites, environmental impact, and finances in mind. By linking already-existing trails on national forest lands, only 180 miles of new trail had to be constructed. The trail follows less-rugged passes and gentler slopes, yet winds among many 14,000-foot peaks, ensuring that it is suitable both for short family hikes and as an access route for climbers.

The trail bypasses many overused mountain sites, avoids disruption of wildlife areas such as elk calving grounds, stays out of avalanche-prone corridors, and skirts fragile meadows and tundra. It passes near several ghost towns in the Sawatch Range, through various life zones, along part of the old Hagerman Railroad route, and into Copper Mountain Ski Area. The trail is as diverse as the mountains through which it travels, and represents the sweat and blisters of hundreds of volunteers who joined ''trail crews'' organized by Gudy Gaskill of the Colorado Mountain Club.

For more Colorado Trail information, contact Friends of the Colorado Trail, 548 Pine Song Trail, Kinnikinnik Hill, Golden, CO· 80401.

which stare at each other across the Front Range.

Edwin James has not been forgotten entirely, however. The beautiful 13,294-foot peak that towers over Winter Park and which is seen by millions each year from Interstate 70 near Genessee bears the name of the first white man to stand on the roof of the Rockies: James Peak.

A short chapter

The era of mountain men was a short chapter in the story of life among the mountains, begun and ended in less than the lifetime of a good pack mule—the years from 1821 to 1845.

Prior to 1821, land west of the Divide was Spanish soil, technically closed to trade. But when Mexico won its independence, the door of trade was opened and through it rode a breed of men

who left their blaze marks on mountains and the mountain spirit.

Beaver brought them here. High-topped beaver hats were fashionable in centers like London, Paris, and New York and the demand brought $6 a beaver pelt. Huge trapping companies such as the Hudson's Bay Company, the American Fur Company, and the Rocky Mountain Fur Company employed teams of trappers who swarmed every Colorado stream and sidecreek, checking the ground for signs of beaver and the air for the smell of money.

Antoine Robidoux built one collection point, or ''fort,'' along the Gunnison River, while other forts sprang up at Taos, along the Arkansas River, and at Brown's Hole in the Uintas along the Green River.

At the heart of this era, though, was another breed of men, ''free trappers.'' These were the mountain men of legend: Jim ''Ol' Gabe'' Bridger, Bill Williams M.T.—the initials stood for ''Master Trapper,'' a self-appointed title—Kit Carson, and Thomas ''Broken Hand'' Fitzpatrick. Some who were most active in Colorado have been forgotten, men like John Hatcher, Uncle Dick Wooten, Calvin Briggs, and William Wolfskill. Others, like Louis Vasquez, are remembered only by names such as Vasquez Peaks on Colorado maps.

Many of these free trappers began with large fur companies before trapping for themselves, combing the mountains alone for most of the year, dependent only on their Hawken rifles, their Bowie knives, and their wits for survival. They were men with a past best left behind, or with a thick streak of independence. They liked their horizons filled with nothing but more horizons.

Free trappers were men like Mariano Medina who spoke thirteen Indian dialects and married a Flathead Indian woman after trading a few horses and a blanket for her. Medina was shot six different times and became "ugly medicine" to the Indians.

James Baker, another free trapper, claimed to have visited every valley in the Colorado Rockies and never carried cooking gear. He'd kill a deer, take only the ribs, prop them bone side to a fire, and eat off them until they spoiled. He was a handsome man, described as "gentle as a child when used rightly, a wounded grizzly when provoked," and once joined Jim Bridger in attacking a pair of grizzlies, armed with only a knife, just for the sport of it. He was a quiet man, "not broke to civilization," and the collection of the Colorado Historical Museum contains one of hundreds of beaver pelts brought out of the mountains by Jim Baker.

The mountain men came together in July of 1825 for the first of the great "rendezvous" along the Green River in the Uintah Range. The gathering was an idea of William Ashley, a kingpin in the fur trade. Rather than wait for trappers to bring furs to his fort, Ashley decided, his fort would go to the trappers.

The annual event brought mountain men out of the hills to trade, drink, fight, and tell stories. The "Taos Lightning" liquor at one rendezvous, the Santa Fe *Republican* reported, was "none of your old stuff neither, but bran new, lacking six days of being a week old." There was killing. Indian women for sale were paraded on ponies with bells around their necks. And at one point, more business was conducted during a rendezvous along the Green River than at the business centers of Taos and Bents Fort.

It was a heady time, but it was not to last. In 1832, the first silk hat caught the eyes of the fashion world. Beaver went out of style. A pelt which brought $6 at the height of the era was worth only $1 by 1838. Increasingly, Indian raids made trapping more dangerous for less return. And Colorado's creeks had been all but trapped out anyway.

The last rendezvous occurred in 1840, just fifteen years after the first. Slowly, forts were abandoned or burnt to the ground. William Bent, who built a fort on the banks of the Arkansas River, blew it up in disgust one night in 1849. There was no stopping the end of the era and the mountain men, not bent on ceremony or long goodbyes, simply rode away.

Straight through the heart

Somewhere out on the broad expanse of the San Luis Valley, John Charles Fremont stopped on December 7, 1848. His expedition had come up the Arkansas River, crossed the Wet Mountains and the Sangre de Cristo Range in five inches of snow, skirted the Great Sand Dunes, and reached the doorstep of the San Juan Mountains. He was faced with a decision on the route through the mountains. That decision, made while camped in the San Luis Valley, led Fremont's party to disaster.

Fremont had been a hero. His three previous expeditions between 1840 and 1847 had won him honor, rank, and fame. But by autumn 1848, a court-martial and his abrupt resignation from the U.S. Army had tarnished his reputation, a reputation he hoped to earn back on a privately funded expedition to survey the 38th parallel from St. Louis to San Francisco in search of a route for the Transcontinental Railway.

Fremont, with 33 men and 120 mules, reached Pueblo in November of 1848, at the onset of a bad winter. He hoped to cross the mountains in winter, thereby rekindling his fame as the "pathfinder" and to test the winter viability of the route. Men like Uncle Dick Wooten, mountain men who could read the signs of the approaching winter, warned Fremont to wait for spring. Then Fremont discovered that his trusted guide, Kit Carson, was bed-ridden in Taos and unavailable for the expedition. But instead of waiting, Fremont hired "Old Bill" Williams, who had served as one of the guides for Fremont's third expedition in 1845. The new party gathered 130 bushels of corn as reserve rations and pushed ahead.

Somewhere around a sagebrush campfire on the windy flats of the San Luis Valley, Williams and Fremont argued about the route. Williams, who knew the country well, wanted to use Cochetopa Pass just to the north, which was a known winter route, or to swing south along the Old Spanish Trail. Fremont, having glimpsed the San Juans from the top of the pass in the Sangres, had a different plan: straight through the heart.

They followed the Rio Grande beyond the present-day site of Del Norte and on December 11 camped at Alder Creek. There, on Dec. 12, the party started up Alder Creek, probably fifteen miles short of their intended route up Willow Creek. They ran head-on into Mesa Mountain.

The snows around the mountain were four feet deep and crusted with ice. With each step the mules sank to their saddles and sliced their forelegs until the snow was webbed with blood. The men used mauls made from tree limbs to pound a path in the snow. The work was painfully slow and exhausting. On Dec. 15, eight mules died of exhaustion.

The next day, seven more mules died, slowing the party more by forcing men to carry heavy loads on their backs. More snow fell. The expedition camped just three miles from the camp of the previous night but within sight of what they thought was the Continental Divide.

Mules were dying where they stood, or chewing up their blankets and saddle pads to stay alive. Finally, on Dec. 17, the party managed to push a trail over the ridge, only to come face-to-face with a sea of endless peaks and the awful reality of being lost. They had simply scaled a spur ridge, not the Divide. At the headwaters of Wanamaker

Creek, a storm pinned them down for six long, hard days.

They could not go forward, and trails they had pounded behind them were drifted in, useless. So Fremont's expedition turned to a new route southeast down Embargo Creek. Days passed, more mules died, and men, exhausted, teetered on the edge of collapse. On Christmas Day, they dug a hole in the snow with pots and pans to form "Camp Hope," and the men shared a Christmas feast of "Fried Mule, Broiled Mule, Stewed Mule and Water."

Frostbite chewed the fingers, toes, and faces of the men and hunger clawed at their insides. Four men, including Williams and Henry King, the powerful squad leader, were sent down the Rio Grande River for help. The rest of the party staggered and crawled behind.

Fremont made the Rio Grande on January 2, but part of *his* group remained far behind up Embargo Creek. Food was low, and most of the mules were now buried by snow far up the mountain. More than a week passed and no rescue party had returned. Fremont gathered another volunteer group.

Leaving the river and the other twenty-four men, Fremont and four companions set out on their own for help. On January 16, they came upon "the most miserable objects," three survivors of the original rescue party. They had eaten their last "food"—a few candles—three days after leaving the main party, and since no game was moving in the cold, had been forced to roast and eat their boots, stumbling forward down the river by day, sleeping in the snow at night. Eventually, the fourth member of the rescue party, Henry King, urged the others on, lay down in the snow, and died. The remaining three ate his body.

That was when Fremont found them. Four days later, the combined rescue parties reached a settlement on the Red River and assembled a team to go back for the others. By the time they returned to the expedition, two men had abandoned the

main party. Neither survived. One, begging to be shot, had turned back towards an old camp and was left to die. The other had lost his mind, wandered aimlessly, and ranted about food until he drifted away from the main party and was never seen again. Other men in the main party had gone snowblind. Those who could had hunted and killed two grouse. Another ate part of a dead wolf. Still another ate bugs and rosebuds. Slowly, more of them had died.

The rescue party collected what little remained of Fremont's expedition into the heart of the San Juans. Ten men had been lost, all 120 of the mules had perished, and most of the equipment had been ruined or abandoned. Yet within two days, Fremont and many of his men were back on the trail, taking a more southerly route towards California.

Five years later, on his last major expedition, Fremont again found himself on the windy flats of the San Luis Valley with a decision to make. This time, though, he routed his men north over Cochetopa Pass and avoided the jagged heart of the Colorado Rockies in the winter.

Gold and ghosts

A decade before the discovery of gold in Colorado, Fremont had watched a day end on Colorado's peaks. The sun was setting. Hunters were back in camp and things were quieting down for the night. Deep in the mountains, he wrote in his journal, "The whole valley is glowing and bright and all the mountains are gleaming like silver."

Although this passage refers only to the colors of a mountain sunset, Fremont knew the signs of color in rocks as well. He mentions the mineral potential of Colorado's mountains several times in his published journals. But Fremont's hints went unheeded. The mountains of Colorado were considered mostly a wasteland in the 1840s and early 1850s, nothing but a little-known extension of the Kansas Territory.

Today, at the spot where the South Platte River

is joined by the waters of Cherry Creek, the horizons are hemmed in by Denver skyscrapers. In 1858, though, when gold was discovered in gravel here, Pikes Peak might have been visible on the southwestern horizon a hundred miles distant. And it didn't matter that the electrifying discovery was not made at the foot of Pikes Peak, for "Pikes Peak or Bust" became the rallying cry of a new gold rush.

In 1858, when gold was discovered in Colorado, the California rush of 1849 had fizzled for all but a lucky few. A cycle of unemployment and recession was devastating the cities of the East. So waves of wagons were crossing the prairies from both directions, carrying the dreams and fates of an estimated 100,000 people and converging on the new promised land, the Colorado mountains.

Those first lucky prospectors on Cherry Creek had tapped into the northeastern tip of a swath of gold, silver, and other precious minerals. As others arrived, too late to stake claims near the original find, they spread out and began to outline "the ribbon of gold," Colorado's mineral belt.

Cherry Creek was first in 1858. Other strikes defined the belt to the south and west—Gregory Gulch in the Front Range in 1859; Breckenridge in the Tenmile Range and Fairplay in the Mosquito Range, both also in 1859; Tin Cup in the Sawatch Range in 1861; the big find at Silverton in the Needles in 1870; Lake City in 1871; Telluride in the San Juans in 1875; and Aspen in the Elk Mountains during 1879. The belt took shape as a fifty-mile-wide zone extending southwest from the Front Range to the San Juans. Some miners were trained in geology. Some had been through the California Gold Rush. Many followed leads given in the Hayden Atlas. In one section of the Sawatch Range considered promising by Hayden, who led the 1872 Hayden Survey into the region, seven camps were erected by 1875.

Other miners were just lucky. One made the strike at Bachelor while searching for a rock to toss at his stubborn mule. A hunter saw shiny rocks at what became the Buckskin Joe Mine while following the blood trail of a deer he had wounded.

Whether by luck or skill, the region rapidly became the state's money belt. Most minerals mined in Colorado have come from within this area. In just the eight years from 1859 to 1867, $5 million in gold showed up in the pans of placer miners in Summit County alone; another $5 million during the same time was taken from Lake County. An even richer payload was hauled out of Gregory Gulch—$9 million during that same run of luck. Yet even those figures are pocket change compared to big finds at the one major exception to the mineral belt boundaries, a place called Cripple Creek.

The small, more-rocks-than-water creek that flows off the south flank of Pikes Peak was, until 1890, just a nuisance to local ranchers whose cattle broke their legs trying to cross the poor excuse for a stream that the locals called Cripple Creek. But in that year, two sheepherders picked up some strange, highly flecked rocks near the creek and the boom was on.

Nearly half of all the gold and silver mined in Colorado has come from the Cripple Creek mines. Since the strike, ironically first made in a place called Poverty Gulch, more than 2 million ounces of silver and nearly 19 million ounces of gold have been recovered. Gold flowed like the waters of the tiny creek never did. In one year alone, 1900, $18 million in gold was scratched from the hills, and an estimated $450 million in all has been produced. The area was so rich that Bennett Avenue, one of the main streets of Cripple Creek, was paved with leftover gold ore the miners didn't think worth the effort to process.

The success stories have been often told, the riches counted over and over again. But the rush for gold left another legacy among the mountains, too. For every strike made, there were many misses. For every fortune made, a hundred

Clouds sift through trees on the Skyline Ranch in the San Juans. W. PERRY CONWAY

dreams died. The mountains are dotted with the wooden skeletons of those dreams, now called ghost towns.

Standing on dirt streets in places like Eureka or St. Elmo or Ashcroft today, less than a century after they were built, the air still seems to echo with laughter, gunfire, and the sounds of a saloon's piano. Breezes still seem to carry the scents of cigars, horses, and sweat.

These towns once reflected the thrills of quick fortunes. Bachelor, a town that dug $800,000 in silver during one month in 1893 and is now nothing but slates of weathered wood, had three businesses—two saloons and a parlor house. Adelaide, in the Sawatch Range, had thirty-six cabins, twenty-eight mining- oriented businesses, and four saloons.

Mining towns lived fast and died hard. Many were built high, in keeping with a miners' creed that, "A good silver mine is found above timberline ten times out of nine." At such high altitudes, however, avalanches plagued the towns. A slide which rumbled into Tomichi in the mountains west of Gunnison in 1899, trapping six men and a dog, spelled the end of that town. It was a common fate.

Other towns died by fire. Flames devastated Cripple Creek twice in five days and Placerville, Garfield, and Whitehorn also burned. Sometimes residents rebuilt their town, and sometimes they just moved.

Death was much slower for many towns. The wind blowing through the wooden hallways of Alpine at Chalk Creek, on the flanks of Mt. Princeton, sounds today like the wailing of a far-off train, a train that reached only as far as St. Elmo three miles upstream and left Alpine—which by 1880 had five hundred residents, a newspaper, and twenty-three saloons—to die. Such was the fate of hundreds of forgotten towns. Dreams died, too, and today the streets are walked only by wind, and nothing but silence is golden.

High science

From a distance, Gothic looks no different than scores of other ghost towns haunting the Colorado mountains. The wood of old buildings has the same weathered gray cast. Small, colored ribbons offer the first clues that Gothic is different. The ribbons define a quadrant used to study contrasting patterns of reproduction in native plant species, or a tiny mousetrap used in a thirty-year small mammal census. The next clue might not be so subtle—the sight of 175 scientists from around the country who bring this "ghost" town to life every spring.

The population of 175 scientists is not much compared with more than 8,000 people who lived here in the East River Valley between the Elk and West Elk mountains during Gothic's silver boom. Then, in the 1870s, it had more than 170 buildings including three hotels, a school, and four newspapers. But today, the town has the nation's foremost high-altitude biological field station.

By the time silver hit bottom in 1893, Gothic was already played out. Avalanches, the threat of Indian raids, and plummeting silver prices drove most folks out by 1884, and the town was on its way to oblivion. Then, in 1928, the site caught the eye of Dr. John C. Johnson from Western State College in Gunnison. He bought the townsite for back taxes which totalled $200 and offered an extra $3 for the twenty-two-room hotel. The Rocky Mountain Biological Laboratory (RMBL) was born.

Although the townsite is only 250 acres by itself, it is surrounded by the 1.7-million-acre Gunnison National Forest and the 175,000-acre Maroon Bells-Snowmass Wilderness Area.

Perhaps even more important, the site serves as a natural laboratory. Studies focus on ecosystems. They range from the aquatic habitat of the East River on the valley floor to the wind-swept alpine tundra at over 13,000 feet. Gothic sits at a kind of confluence where plant and animal species from the Great Basin, High Plains, mountains, and canyon country of the southwest come together.

People who come here are as diverse as the ecosystems they study. Some, like Dr. Paul Ehrlich who has been studying butterflies here for twenty years, are nationally known. Others are college undergraduates participating in summer field courses. Since the RMBL is a private, non-profit entity not affiliated with any one university, scientists themselves must pay the bills for independent research projects. Funds for work investigating everything from the wing color patterns of butterflies to predation among river insects comes from sources such as the National Geographic Society, the Mellon Foundation, various universities, and the National Science Foundation. More than four hundred scientific papers have been published based on the findings of research done at the old ghost town.

What was once just another forgotten mining town is now exposing the inner workings of life in the mountains, showing man his place in those mountains. Right across from the Old Town Hall sits a solar-heated log laboratory looking as natural as the wooden outhouses. But inside are rows of the most modern computers for data analysis and rooms filled with shiny, new laboratory equipment. Two very different worlds meet in Gothic. But some things never change, and late at night when butterfly nets and data books are put aside, laughter from the mess hall rings through the dirt streets just the way it did a century ago when the miners of Gothic put down their picks and shovels and gathered around the tables at the Old Gothic Hotel.

The vertical dance

It was late, 11:15 p.m., when Albert Ellingwood and Eleanor Davis made their way back into camp on the banks of Spanish Creek in the Sangre de Cristo Range. The day, July 24, 1916, had been one to remember, filled with grand vistas and mountain summits. Now, as they rested around the campfire, the day had come to an end, and so had an era. The trio of peaks around their base camp had just become the last 14,000-foot summits in the Colorado Rockies to be climbed.

Ellingwood, Davis, and five others came to the Sangre de Cristos in search of "peaks unclimbed and peaks unclimbable." Ellingwood, a professor at Princeton University and a Rhodes Scholar who learned to climb in England's Lake District, was one of the premier climbers in the Rocky Mountains with history-making climbs in both the Teton and Wind River ranges of Wyoming.

First, from a camp on Willow Creek, they had scaled 14,165-foot Kit Carson Peak. Then, moving their base camp to nearby Spanish Creek, the strongest climbers in the party had topped 14,294-foot Crestone Peak. On the same day, while the others headed for the comforts of camp, Ellingwood and Davis had traversed the ridge separating Crestone Peak from 14,191-foot Crestone Needle. When the two reached camp that evening, every 14,000-foot summit in Colorado had known the footprints of man.

Climbing began early in Colorado. Artifacts found atop some peaks indicate that Indians climbed for several reasons including religious ceremonies, hunting, and warfare. Miners poked holes at or near summits looking for riches. An interview with a miner in 1867 told of workers at the West Argentine Mine who, after "solemnly wearing away rock all day and playing poker for tobacco all night," would climb to the 14,267-foot summit of Torreys Peak to observe the Sabbath.

Distant Peaks

Carl Blaurock, 92, talks with his hands weaving the air as if searching for a handhold, his eyes looking far off as if picking a route. He is a mountain man whose life has included more Colorado highcountry than any other living person. Born April 22, 1896, his first climb was of Pikes Peak in 1909 with his father.

In 1912, Blaurock joined an organization only a few weeks old, the Colorado Mountain Club, where he learned from the best climbers of the day. In 1920, atop 14,083-foot Mount Eolus in the San Juans, Blaurock and climbing partner Bill Ervin shook hands on a promise to climb every 14,000-foot Colorado peak.

In those days, just reaching the San Juans was "like an expedition." They hopped the Denver & Rio Grande Railroad in 1921, paused at the whistle-stop town of Blanca to climb Mount Lindsey and Culebra Peak, and then hopped back on the train for Creede.

They talked an old prospector at the lonely Equity Mine into putting them up, after satisfying him that they were not revenue agents out to break up bootlegging operations. In two weeks they climbed nine high peaks, covering two hundred miles on foot. And within three years after shaking hands, the two men sat atop 14,165-foot Kit Carson Peak in the Sangre de Cristo Range and shook hands again, the first people to scale all Colorado's highest peaks.

In July of 1973, 77-year-old Carl Blaurock made the last of his major climbs, scaling Notch Mountain. In sixty-four years of climbing, he had led scores of climbs for the Colorado Mountain Club, often stuffing newspapers in his clothing to stay warm. In 1926, he slid fifteen hundred feet down the face of St. Vrain Glacier. And he helped retrieve the body of his friend Agnes Vaille, one of the early woman mountaineers, who died during a blizzardous winter climb up the East Face of Longs Peak.

The sorrow remains. But Carl Blaurock, his hand around a glass of homemade chokecherry brandy, recalls happier climbs, too, and the sweetness of a life spent on Colorado's peaks.

The men of government surveys trudged up countless peaks in the name of science. In the early 1860s, C.C. Parry, one of the eminent botanists of his time, lugged a barometer up mountains like Pikes Peak, Mount Audubon, Grays and Torreys peaks, James Peak, Mount Guyot, Mount Flora, and the peak which would eventually bear his own name, Parry Peak. Using his barometer, Parry recorded the most accurate elevation readings of the time for these peaks. Several of his climbs were first ascents; several of those peaks were named by Parry. Yet this energetic scientist many called "the king of Colorado botany" is best remembered in the names of mountain flowers like Parry's primrose, Parry's penstemon, and Parry's larkspur.

Another scientist, better remembered for rivers than for mountains, also had his hand in early mountaineering history—Major John Wesley Powell. In 1868, Powell and six others including William Byers, founder of the *Rocky Mountain News,* became the first white party to scale Longs Peak, reaching the summit on August 23. Placing their names in a tin can left on the summit, the Major gave a speech, perhaps foreshadowing his historic Grand Canyon voyage, calling for the same success on "mountains more formidable in other fields of effort."

In the same year, Powell racked up another first by ascending the highest peak in the Gore Range, 13,534-foot Mount Powell. Near the summit of that peak, according to one member of the party, the climbing got a bit difficult for the one-armed Major. "At one time we became separated by my climbing where the Major could not follow with his one hand," wrote Ned Farnell; "...it seemed too hazardous for a one-armed man to go further...but he would not give up and we cautiously moved on, passing many places where a single misstep or a slip of the foot would be certain death."

The Major was undoubtedly a courageous explorer and leader. He was not, it seems, much of a camp cook. There at the summit of Mount Powell, one of the men left a biscuit baked by the Major, claiming it was so hard it would stand even the most wicked mountain weather and remain "an everlasting tribute."

In 1896 the Rocky Mountain Club was formed, and in 1912 the Colorado Mountain Club began with its publication, *Trail and Timberline,* which became the chronicler of mountain climbing history in the state. To this day *Trail and Timberline,* along with William Bueler's book, *Roof of the Rockies,* remains the most respected source of mountain climbing history.

That history changed directions after Ellingwood and Davis stood atop the last unclimbed 14,000-foot peak in the state. Ironically, Ellingwood himself pushed the sport of mountain climbing in its new direction.

In 1924, Ellingwood returned to the Sangre de Cristo Range and a ridge on the northeast side of Crestone Peak. Angling at 55 degrees for 2,000 feet, this wall dropping directly from the summit offered a significantly more challenging route than he had climbed eight years earlier. The climb of what became known as the "Ellingwood Arete" showed that mountain climbing was no longer simply a matter of reaching summits. *Routes* became more important than summits. Mountain climbing became an artform, what Colorado climber Rick Medrick has called "the vertical dance."

On no Colorado peak has the dance been more breathtaking than on the east face of Longs Peak—the "Diamond." Like a chisel cut in the side of Longs Peak, the Diamond is a 945-foot sheer wall. Climbers stood below its dizzying height looking for routes up its glass-smooth surface for years. Until 1960 they could only look because the Diamond, by order of the National Park Service, was "off limits."

In 1960, that order was rescinded. By the third day of August that same year, Robert Kamps and David Rearick, after once being driven back by bad weather and spending a cold night on a two-foot wide ledge, had "done" the Diamond.

Since the legend fell, others have pioneered new routes up the Diamond. Some climbed it with less gear. It was climbed in winter (Kor and Goss, 1967). It was climbed solo (Forrest, 1970). Each time, the possibilities of mountain climbing grew. There are no great summits left unclimbed in Colorado, but now personal, inner territory is being explored, the summits of the self.

Colorado still offers a whole gamut of climbing opportunities—from the walk up 14,000-footers of the Sawatch Range to glacier

The angel of Shavano

In mid-summer—July in a snowy year—in late afternoon or on cloudy days, the southeast face of Mount Shavano in the Sawatch Range seems almost to take flight.

The peak faces U.S. Highway 285 between Buena Vista and Salida. As winter fades from the Sawatch Range, snow clinging to cracks in the face of Mount Shavano etches the soft outline of an angel overlooking the valley with outstretched arms.

Once South Park, below the peak, was an important hunting and farming ground for Indian tribes. According to Indian legend, an Indian princess watched suitors come to her, offering gifts of precious rocks, grizzly claws, the finest hides, and the choicest crops. She watched with no expression on her beautiful face as young warriors battled to prove their love for her. Nothing they did melted her heart of ice.

Because of her coldness, the gods turned her into an ice angel on the face of Mount Shavano, to remain there until something stirred her deeply, bringing emotion to her cold heart.

There she stayed, appearing each summer to look down on her people in the valley. One year, the rains did not come and the skies were dry as dust. Rivers choked and hid themselves in the rocks. Corn shriveled and turned brown. People began to grow thin and die, their bones turning to dust and blowing away. Children stopped playing and searched for rocks to put in their mouths to slake the thirst.

Seeing this, the Angel grew sad for her people and began to cry. Her warm tears melted the ice and the waters ran down into the valley, replenishing the rivers and bringing life back to the crops. Leaves in the trees blew in the cool wind with the sounds of running water. Children came outside to play again and game returned to the hunters.

To this day, says the legend, the Angel of Shavano returns to the face of this mountain each summer to look down and bless the valley where her people so long ago were saved by a princess who learned the value of emotion.

White thunder

Colorado's mountains rumble with more than 20,000 avalanches every winter, making the state the most avalanche-prone in the nation. Many occur in remote areas posing no danger to human life or property. Others are triggered intentionally to pre-empt danger. The avalanche at left was triggered with "Avalauncher" explosives on Feb. 21, 1986, because it threatened a road to the AMAX mine south of Berthoud Pass. Originating near the top of 12,521-foot Mt. Stanley, this avalanche roared nearly five thousand feet downhill, probably exceeding 100 mph.

There are two types of avalanches—loose snow avalanches and deeper slab slides. A loose snow avalanche begins in dry, powdery snow, growing as it descends in cloud-like fashion and stabilizing after the run. A slab slide begins as a large area of snow fractures in heavier, densely packed snow, reaches full power within seconds, and remains unstable even after the run.

Snow accumulating faster than an inch an hour increases the potential for avalanches greatly. Rapid changes in temperature, especially if associated with drastic wind shifts, can also destabilize snow. Avalanches are most common on slopes of 30-45 degrees and forested slopes are safer than open slopes. Be alert for freshly run avalanche chutes and hollow or "woofing" sounds in the snowpack. Look for long cracks or fracture lines. And be aware of the snow crystal makeup, since small, icy, needle- or pellet-like snowflakes are more often associated with avalanche danger than classic star-shaped snowflakes.

If an avalanche does occur, discard ski poles and other equipment. Move with swimming motions to stay near the surface, and as the slide slows, cover your mouth with your hand to make an air space. Try to remain calm and make noises or motions to aid in rescue. D. BACHMAN

climbing in Rocky Mountain National Park. More than 6 million people have stood on the summit of Pikes Peak, a record for major peaks second only to Fujiyama in Japan—and most of them *drove* there on the Pikes Peak Highway. Within a few hours' drive it is possible to climb alone for days in the Gore Range. Eldorado Canyon near Boulder has become a national center for climbers attracted not to peaks but to the challenge of routes and personal skills. Organizations like the Colorado Mountain Club, Colorado Outward Bound, and Outdoor Leadership Training Seminars sponsor classes and trips in the San Juan, Gore, Needle, and Front ranges.

Any kind of climbing is a personal statement of freedom. Paul Sibley, who runs a climbing school in Eldorado Canyon, says a mountainside is a place where "the only rules and regulations are the most basic ones; gravity and your own skill." The best climbers, says Sibley, "are those striving to become a part of the mountain rather than trying to conquer it."

Colorado's mountains may have been climbed, but they will never be conquered. Mountains are too much for that. Mankind has been learning that lesson, slowly, since the first lone figure sat in stillness atop Old Man Mountain with his offering of obsidian. ■

A mountain sketchbook

In 1972, the first of five Landsat satellites was launched, providing scientists with an unprecedented bird's-eye view of the earth's surface. High-resolution photographs taken from 570 miles in the sky show 12,000 square miles of the earth's surface in each frame. Scientists in the Earth Resource Department at Colorado State University have spliced together frames of Colorado and created a portrait of the mountains never before possible. At first glance, only a few landmarks stand out from the composite photo—the long, thin Sangre de Cristos, the protrusion of Pikes Peak. Closer inspection, though, reveals the patterns of Colorado's mountain ranges, as rough and furrowed as bark.

This is a landscape rippling with ranges. Colorado contains more than forty recognized ranges, but precise counts are impossible. Coloradans disagree, for example, on whether the Needles,

La Platas, La Garitas, San Miguels, and Grenadiers belong to the San Juan Range or are individual ranges. And geologists do not consider the San Juan Mountains a range at all, but a "massif"—a mountainous area of relatively uniform geologic structure. A "range," to a geologist, is a geographically definable linear formation of peaks. By this definition, the Sangre de Cristos, Tenmiles, and Gores are ranges; the San Juans, Elks, and Flattops are not.

Many of today's "ranges" were named by trappers, mountain men, climbers, or explorers, people who knew less about geology or taxonomy than about the landscape surrounding them. To them, a "range" was defined by the view from the highest local summit or by a day's pack trip.

The following sketches, arranged in alphabetical order, portray well-known and little-known ranges, those which dominate satellite

photographs and those which a trapper, on a good day, could hike from tip to tail. These are Colorado's mountain ranges.

Culebra Range

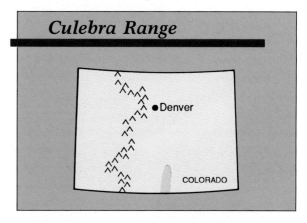

Highest Point: Culebra Peak (14,069 feet).
Other Major Peaks: Purgatory Peak (13,676 feet),
  Trinchera Peak (13,517 feet), Mariquita (13,405 feet).
Cities: Stonewall, Monument Park, Cucharas.
Counties: Costilla, Huerfano, Las Animas.
Public Land: San Isabel National Forest.

The Culebra Range slithers into Colorado from New Mexico, curving near its center like a snake basking in the sun. Perhaps the Spanish gold-seekers who followed these mountains into Colorado saw the resemblance, or perhaps they saw snakes on the hillsides. Either way, this range running thirty miles south from La Veta Pass to the state line in southeastern Colorado has for centuries been known as Culebra, "the snake."

This hot, dry range rises out of the dusty plains like a mirage. At its center and southern end, dark igneous peaks set it apart from the Sangre de Cristo Range to the north, ripping through treeline to catch rainclouds and cool winds. Humans visited these summits early and artifacts like hand-chipped projectile points have been found far above timberline. Its proximity to the plains made it one of the first Colorado ranges to be explored.

Sunset sets Colorado's mountains afire.
TOM TROGDON

As early as the sixteenth-century, Spanish explorers left a trail of names like Culebra, Mariquita, Quatro, Francisco, and Trinchera as they followed this range into southeastern Colorado looking for gold. Some gold was found, or so the legends say, but something just as valuable was also found—water. Early attempts at settlements occurred all along the gently sloping eastern side of the Culebra Range where the St. Charles River flows out of the hills. And today, partly as a result of those early settlements, most of the Culebra Range is privately owned. The northern peaks of the range, from Mount Maxwell to Raspberry Mountain and now within the boundaries of San Isabel National Forest, are among the only peaks of the Culebra Range on public property.

On the northeastern tip of the range, just east of La Veta Pass, sits long, thin Mount Mestas. A rock glacier slips slowly down its side, evidence of the continuing work of erosion. Huge talus slopes, lubricated by ice and water trapped underneath, chew patiently into the mountainside like ice glaciers.

The more rugged west side of the Culebras was sliced by the same fault which caused the jagged edge of the Sangre de Cristo Range to the north. In the Culebras, that fault has carved steeper terrain surrounding the high peaks in the southwestern part of the range. This western Culebra Range was once a part of the giant Sangre de Cristo Grant deeded in the 1840s to Stephen Lee, who acted both as sheriff and the local bootlegger of "Taos Lightning," and to a 12-year-old boy named Narciso Beaubien. At the time, ownership of lands south of the Arkansas River was being disputed on one side by Texas, which only a few years earlier in 1836 had won its independence from Mexico, and on the other side by New Mexico, which felt the lands were a natural extension of its northern boundary.

To strengthen its claim on the land, New Mexico Governor Manuel Armijo awarded huge tracts of land to nearly anyone who asked for it, as long

as they agreed to settle there. Lee and the boy hardly had a chance to settle, though, before both were killed by Indians. Following a series of other owners, English buyers eventually purchased the grant sight-unseen through a brochure which claimed that, even in winter, the San Luis Valley never gets cold. Large parts of the Culebra Range today are owned by the Forbes Trinchera Ranch.

Off the beaten track, far from the heart of the state and the hearts of tourists, the Culebra Range has been overlooked through most of history. Teddy Roosevelt briefly attracted attention to the range once when he hunted here. And when Franklin D. Roosevelt died, some state legislators wanted to rename Culebra Peak in his honor, even sculpt his likeness in its cliffs. But the state's Democratic leaders argued that renaming a peak in the "Snake" Range would only serve to "provide effective campaign material for Republican orators."

So attention again turned away from the Culebra Range, leaving it to stretch quietly, as it has for millions of years, under the warm sun of southeastern Colorado.

The Elk Mountains

High Point: *Castle Peak (14,265 feet)*.
Other Major Peaks: *South Maroon Peak (14,156 feet), Pyramid Peak (14,018 feet), Snowmass Mountain (14,092 feet), Capitol Peak (14,130 feet), Mt. Sopris (12,953 feet)*.

Cities: *Aspen, Crested Butte, Carondale, Basalt, Paonia.*
Counties: *Gunnison, Pitkin.*
Public Land: *White River and Gunnison national forests, Maroon Bells-Snowmass Wilderness Area, West Elk Wilderness.*

In 1853, Lieutenant E.G. Beckwith, who assumed command of the Gunnison Survey after Indians killed Captain Gunnison in Utah's Great Basin, led the party over Cochetopa Pass toward an unknown mountain range to the northwest. There on the flanks of the pass were "numerous elk horns...scattered whitening on the hills." Thus the Elk Mountains were named. But even as late as 1873, William H. Brewer, second in command of the Whitney expedition, called these mountains "that terra incognito; nameless, untrodden, unknown peaks."

Today, the Elk Mountains rank among the most popular tourist spots in Colorado, a range of exquisite beauty. The landscape, including peaks to the west known locally as the Ruby Range, is a kaleidoscope—Purple Mountain, Maroon Pass, Copper Lake, Raspberry Creek, Crystal Peak, Cinnamon Mountain.

The heart of the range is the Maroon Bells. Towering over Crater Lake, Maroon and North Maroon peaks—both over 14,000 feet high—are elegant examples of mountain beauty. Late Paleozoic sediments hardened by heat and pressure layer the face of the bell-shaped peaks like brush strokes. The sight of the peaks mirrored in the surface of Maroon Lake is one of the most majestic, and most photographed, in the Rocky Mountains.

The snow-etched ridges of North Maroon Peak meant a challenge as well as sublime winter beauty for Fritz Stammberger. In June of 1971, while snow still clung to cracks in the face of North Maroon Peak, Stammberger climbed atop the peak he had climbed solo for the first time that same winter. This time, however, Stammberger wasn't intent on ascending North Maroon Peak. Instead, it was the descent which challenged him—a descent on skis.

Stammberger had already skied slopes of the Himalayas' Cho Oyu, seventh-highest peak in the world. In the Maroon Bells, he carefully plotted a route connecting the white stripes of snow on ledges, then reviewed that route as he climbed. Once on top of the mountain, he turned around and skied down the face of North Maroon Peak in just forty-eight minutes.

Skiing of another sort still brings international attention to the Elk Range. Aspen, at the northeastern edge of the range, and Crested Butte in the south are both well-known ski towns. Once faced with extinction like so many towns which boomed across the Elk Range during the mining era, both now thrive on "white gold," the snows of the Elks. The Maroon Bells-Snowmass Wilderness encompasses some of the best cross-country ski routes in the West, threading among six 14,000-foot peaks which form the crest of the Elk Range.

These same high peaks have long attracted climbers to the Elk Range. Members of the Hayden Survey of the 1870s made several first ascents here, but also were among the first to discover the dangers of climbing in the Elks. Some peaks, like Castle, are of sturdy granite. Others like the Maroon Bells, though, are composed of brittle, sharp-edged sedimentary rock cracked and shattered by the heat and pressure of nearby volcanic activity. They are mountains, as Hayden put it, in a "state of chaos."

The rock in places is so loose that one member of an 1873 climb of Snowmass guessed that "an industrious man, with a crow bar, could, by a week's industrious exertion, reduce the height of the mountain by one or two hundred feet." On that climb, the writer reported that the party "amused themselves" by rolling huge boulders off the face of the mountain. But loose rocks kicked free by climbers above, slips on ledges covered with tiny, ball-bearing-type pebbles, and rock falls on talus slopes have taken their toll in injury and death to climbers through the years. The same forces which created the graceful beauty of the Elk Range have also earned them a less-than-amusing reputation among climbers as "the deadly bells."

Near the western edge of the range is a mountain with a heart of snow-white marble—Treasure Mountain. First quarried in the late 1800s, this rock from the Elk Mountains was used for the thirty-six pillars, each forty-six feet high and seven feet around, which hold up the Lincoln Memorial in Washington.

The Castles, left, recall one description of the Elk Range by a member of the nineteenth-century Wheeler Survey—"a line of ancient castles" which required "little power of imagination to conceive himself within the ruins of some majestic cathedral." The Anthracite Range, part of the Elks, is in the background. GARY SPRUNG/ GNURPS PHOTOGRAPHY

The same colorful rock which gives the Elks their beauty makes them dangerous to climb. Loose slate and boulder piles have taken their toll on climbers. Yet, climbers do challenge the Elks and Hagerman Peak, right, was named for Percy Hagerman who, along with climbing partner Harold Clark, made first ascents of formidable Elk Range summits like Capitol, North Maroon, and Pyramid peaks. ROBERT BASSE

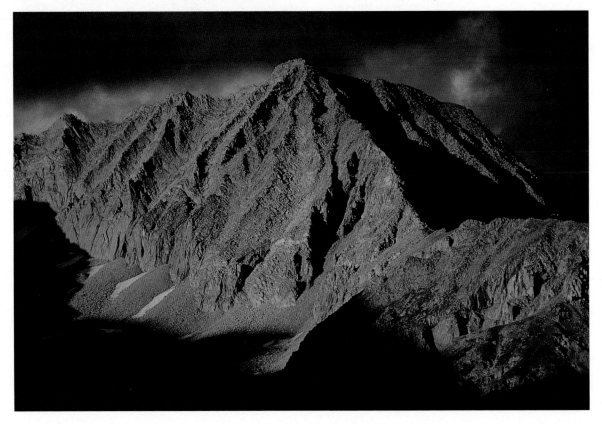

Fed by the deep snows of the Elk Range, the Crystal River, right, flows through Lead King Basin beneath the shadow of Snowmass Mountain. A huge snowfield clings to the eastern face of the peak long into summer and was responsible for the name Snowmass, given by the Hayden Survey Party. MACON COWLES

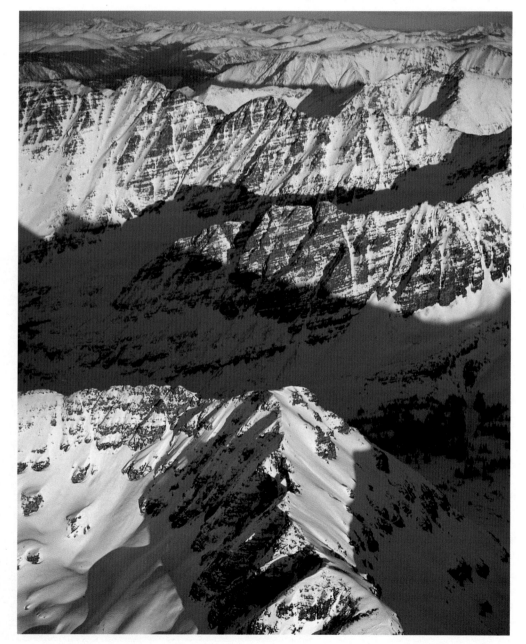

Even more impressive, Treasure Mountain provided the marble for the Tomb of the Unknown Soldier at Arlington National Cemetery. For an entire year, seventy-five men worked to quarry a single block of cool, raw marble that weighed 124 tons. Later, it was trimmed to fifty-six tons measuring fifteen feet long and eight feet high. A crane had to be brought from Vermont to lift it out of the mountain's gut and onto a specially outfitted train car. It took four days to move the marble block four miles to the mill. Then, on November 4, 1932, it was lowered into place at the cemetery—a piece of the cold heart of Colorado's Elk Mountains honoring the nameless heroes who died in World War II.

The sunset colors of the Maroon Bells and the white marble heart of Treasure Mountain place the Elks among the most spectacularly colored ranges in the world. That reputation is reinforced by a southwestern extension known as the Ruby Range. Colors banded in this eight-mile picket-fence extension of the Elk Range have long attracted miners. Hillsides bear the scars of several large mines of the 1880s, and even today a few remnants of the old ways, with their mules and pick-axes, comb the hillsides.

But the future has also come to the Ruby Range. Mt. Emmons, called the ''Red Lady'' by locals, is the target of a large and highly controversial mine which would create a pile as large as Egypt's Aswan Dam.

In contrast, a 5,500-acre section north of the Red Lady has been recommended for inclusion

These snowy ridges of the Elk Range, right, although they may look like western extensions of the massive Sawatch Range on a map, are geologically distinct. Unlike the Sawatch Range, which is made up of faulted anticlines, the Elks were formed by a series of geological processes including a metamorphic stage which produced the deep red colors of many peaks. TOM TILL

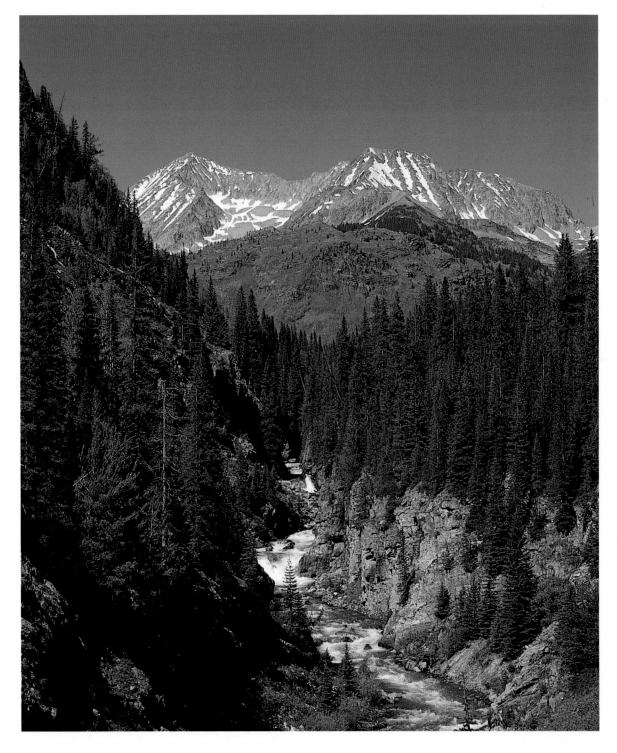

in the National Wilderness Preservation System.

Another mineral, anthracite coal, gives its name to the long, four-mile mountain called the Anthracite Range which separates the Elks from their western extension, the West Elks. The West Elks is a quiet range. Most of its peaks are rounded, wooded, and the highest is West Elk Peak at 13,035 feet. Ringing the range are crowns of volcanic rock known as "breccia," sharpened by wind and rain into spires that look like the teeth of a trap—The Castles and Cathedral Peaks.

Peaks in the West Elks aren't as high as the main range and there are fewer spots of postcard scenery, but thick stands of oakbrush dotted with aspen glens make the West Elks a vital wildlife habitat. Deep stream canyons and open views from peaks like Landsend were protected in the 61,000-acre West Elk Wilderness by the original 1964 Wilderness Act, then expanded to 194,000 acres in 1981.

The Elkhead Range

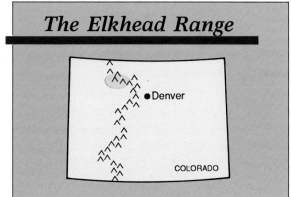

High Point: Welba (10,801 feet).
Other Major Peaks: Mount Oliphant (10,670 feet).
Cities: Craig.
Counties: Routt, Moffat.
Public Land: Routt National Forest.

The Elkhead Range is low and rolling, its peaks barely 10,000 feet high in a state crowded with peaks almost a mile taller. The Elkhead Range is small—even at its widest point a couple of rifle shots stacked end-to-end could clear it. On clear days, Bears Ears Peak, one of the highest mountains of the range, is barely visible as a twin summit north of U.S. Highway 40 near Craig. On windy days, when dust kicks off the unmarked maze of dirt roads converging on Colorado Highway 13, even Welba Peak, the westernmost peak in the Elkheads, the highest and closest peak to a main road, can barely be seen.

Yet the Utes knew where the Elkhead Range was, and this small, eighteen-mile-long range trending east to west in a land of hot canyons and dust proved a vital hunting ground. What rain and snow falls in this dry part of the state collects in pockets of this small range to feed Elk, Little Snake, and Yampa rivers.

Its peaks also made good hide-outs. During the 1870s, the Utes were pushed farther and farther from their native lands. When Nathan Meeker established an Indian Agency just outside the Elkhead Range, tensions grew. Meeker, a driven man, swore to "cut every Indian down to a bare starvation point" if they would not conform to his ways. In an attempt to cure the Indians of what Meeker saw as their lazy ways, he plowed up a field used by Utes for riding competitions and games.

Violence erupted on September 29, 1879, in an unlikely spot—the mouth of Elkhead Creek where it meets the Yampa River after leaving the range. There, a unit of 200 soldiers gathered and defied an order of the Utes by riding down Milk Creek and into the reservation. In the battle that followed, Utes trapped the soldiers in a steep canyon and killed thirteen men, wounded twenty-three, and killed more than 250 pack horses.

That incident escalated into the Meeker Massacre. Back at the Indian Agency, Indians killed Meeker and nine other white men, then took Meeker's wife, his 19-year-old daughter, and two small children hostage into nearby mountains. Although the hostages were released almost a

month later, the incident led to the 1880 Ute Removal Act, which transferred Indians from the mountains of Colorado onto reservations in Utah.

The Elkhead Range itself was produced by violence. Volcanic activity centered around the White River Plateau and the Flattops to the south triggered smaller volcanic eruptions just north of the Yampa River. The Elkhead Range is strewn with evidence of that ancient fire.

It is also strewn with four-wheel-drive roads penetrating the remote corners of the range. Between those roads, however, the wind still blows in small pockets of wilderness.

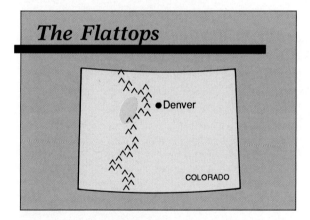

The Flattops

High Point: Flattop Mountain (12,354 feet).
Other Major Peaks: Dome Mountain (12,207 feet),
    Sheep Mountain (12,241 feet).
Cities: Buford, Glenwood Springs, Yampa.
Counties: Garfield, Rio Blanco.
Public Lands: White River National Forest, Flat Tops Wilderness.

Something happened to the Flattops. Rising from broad bases, the peaks reach heights of 11,000 and 12,000 feet and just stop, sheared flat. The sliced look of summits suggests incredible geologic violence but, in fact, the Flattops were caused by quite the opposite.

As the low rumbles of volcanoes in the San Juans were echoing across Colorado's mountains, other volcanoes rose in the smaller White River

Plateau, the center and largest concentration of volcanism in the northern part of the state. Lava pools spread from the vents there to cover many miles. Heat and pressure changed, or "metamorphosized," the native rock in the area, hardening it and setting the stage for the Flattops.

As the land rose—a result of the same uplifts which created the Rocky Mountains—erosion slowly chewed away at softer rocks. Where lava had flowed or rock had been hardened by heat, erosion worked more slowly. Eventually, surrounding landscape was worn away and the flat, hard tops of the Flattops remained.

Unlike any other range in Colorado, the Flattops are a land of pedestals in the air, stages in the sky. The White River Plateau where the Flattops rise is a fifty-mile-long uplift at the doorstep of canyon country. Increased elevation brings more precipitation to the area and the bases of peaks are carpeted with timber and dotted with lakes—Skinny Fish, Surprise, Big Fish, and Paradise. The valleys and hillsides are webbed with creeks—Lynx, Ripple, and Papoose. And both streams and lakes offer some of the best wilderness trout fishing in the state.

Both of the major rivers of northwestern Colorado have their headwaters in the Flattops. Forks flowing off the western side of the range join to form the White River, while the head of the Yampa is located to the east, upstream of the town of Yampa where the growing stream is called the Bear River.

In the center of the Flattops, Trappers Lake resembles most remote wilderness lakes. Beneath towering peaks, green timber surrounds deep blue water. But Trappers Lake has a larger share of mountain history than most wilderness lakes.

In 1918, the U.S. Forest Service sent Arthur Carhart to the lake to survey the area for summer homes. The young "recreational engineer" spent days hiking alone in the mountains nearby and talking around the campfire with other campers and fishermen. An idea was growing. By the time Carhart returned to Denver to submit his report, he was convinced that the best use of Trappers Lake was not as a subdivision for summer homes but as a "wild lands."

The area had been set aside as Colorado's first national forest in 1891. In 1918, when Carhart began efforts to set aside the area as a wilderness, the National Wilderness Preservation System was still half a century away. Carhart's idea was far ahead of its time and received little initial support. Carhart had planted a seed, though, and slowly the concept of wilderness protection gained popularity. When Congress finally created the National Wilderness Preservation System, the 174,000-acre Flat Tops Wilderness Area was among the first in the nation granted wilderness status. In the summer of 1985, the trail circling Trappers Lake was renamed the Arthur C. Carhart Trail, in tribute to one of the fathers of wilderness preservation.

The colossal Chinese Wall in the Flat Tops Wilderness vividly illustrates the distinctive table-like profile of The Flattops, created by cycles of erosion and uplift. The Flat Tops Wilderness was one of the nation's first components of the National Wilderness Preservation System.
CARR CLIFTON

The Front Range

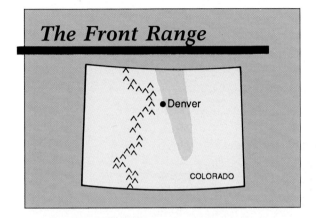

High Point: Grays Peak (14,270 feet).
Other Major Peaks: Torreys Peak (14,267 feet),
  Mount Evans (14,264 feet), Longs Peak (14,255 feet),
  Pikes Peak (14,110 feet), Mount Bierstadt (14,060 feet).

Cities: Estes Park, Boulder, Denver, Colorado Springs.
Counties: Larimer, Boulder, Grand, Gilpin, Park, Douglas,
  Teller, El Paso.
Public Lands: Rocky Mountain National Park, Indian Peaks
  Wilderness, Lost Creek Wilderness, Arapaho, Roosevelt and
  Pike national forests, state and county lands.

New Year's Eve. The sky over Pikes Peak is raining fire. Every December 31 since the 1920s, members of the AdAmAn Club atop Pikes Peak have set the sky ablaze with fireworks visible for miles in all directions.

New Year's Eve. The quiet sky over Longs Peak, a hundred miles north of Pikes Peak, is silver with stars and a sliver of moon. The dark silhouettes of five climbers work their way to the summit. In a few hours, with the climbers watching from the top, the first sun of the new year will rise, lighting the day like a candle.

Two ways to mark the new year. Two very different Front Range mountains. Since 1889, the top of Pikes Peak has been reachable by carriage. Today, the summit is claimed by a road and a railroad and is the finish line for a Fourth of July auto race, marathons, and tourists visiting the nation's highest tourist shop. The summit of Longs Peak, by comparison, is a lonely place. Protected by Rocky Mountain National Park, no roads slice the landscape around this peak.

The differences between Pikes Peak and Longs Peak point out the complex mosaic of mountains comprising Colorado's Front Range. The Front Range is the longest continuous uplift in the state, stretching from the Wyoming border to the Arkansas River. Commonly, however, Coloradans consider the Front Range to be bounded by Longs Peak in the north and Pikes Peak in the south. The land between is a wild array of mountain scenery.

Denver, a small tent city in the 1850s, now boasts its own scenic peaks—skyscrapers of steel and glass, left. Located on the plains at the foot of the Colorado Rockies, Denver's main streets were originally plotted to give pedestrians the best view of mountains such as Mount Evans, the Indian Peaks, Longs Peak, and even Pikes Peak on a clear morning like this one. TIM LUCAS

Trail Ridge Road was opened in 1932 and follows a route used for centuries by Indians into the heart of the Rocky Mountains, right. Longs Peak in the background, 14,255 feet tall, is the highest peak in Rocky Mountain National Park and the northernmost 14,000-foot peak in the Colorado Rockies. W. PERRY CONWAY

The southern border of Rocky Mountain National Park, where Longs Peak is located, is icy and cold, frosted as glass even in summer because of the Indian Peaks. These wild, jagged peaks string the Continental Divide between their summits like a high wire. From Mount Neva to Chiefs Head, most of the named peaks honor the Indian tribes of Colorado—Navajo, Kiowa, Arapaho, Paiute, Arikaree, Pawnee. The tribute was the work of James Grafton Rogers and the Colorado Geographic Board during the early 1900s.

Clinging to wind-blown Niwot Ridge in the Indian Peaks are the high-country scientific stations of the University of Colorado's Institute of Arctic and Alpine Research. Small huts, some of them strapped to the mountainside with cables as thick as a man's wrists against the winds, form the front lines of this world-famous field station. The rustic buildings and modern laboratories of the Mountain Research Station are tucked among trees just below timberline and support classes and research on topics such as acid precipitation, climatic patterns, and alpine flora. This barren finger of land in the Indian Peaks is one of the most thoroughly studied alpine environments in the world.

Toward the center of the Front Range, peaks are higher. Torreys and Grays peaks were named for John Torrey, who began the scientific history of Colorado botany by classifying the collections of the Long Expedition, and Asa Gray, who with Torrey published the first definitive work on North American botany.

In the 1800s, these two classically shaped peaks were among the most famous mountains in the state. An early pack trail winding to the top of Grays Peak made a summit ride a fashionable summer outing among the traveling class. It was, according to one early travel agent, "the best peak for the ladies to visit and the most magnificent peak with the least labor." During that time, Grays was thought to be the highest in the state, an honor which has at various times been bestowed upon Capitol Peak, Pikes Peak, Mount Lincoln, Mount Blanca, Mount Harvard, Mount Sopris, and others. Today that distinction belongs to Mount Elbert in the Sawatch Range.

Initially, artwork drew the interest of the world to the Colorado Rockies, and one of the greatest early landscape artists was Albert Bierstadt. Several times in the 1860s, Bierstadt sat in the shadow of what he called the "Chicago Mountains," one of which would later bear his name, and sketched the beginnings of paintings which have hung in the halls of Congress and in galleries around the East and in Europe. One of his most famous works, "Storm in the Rockies, Mount

Longs Peak, here bathed in alpenglow, is visible for a hundred miles east and led waves of explorers, trappers, miners, and settlers across the plains. Once thought unclimbable, the summit of Longs Peak is now the goal of 10,000 climbers annually, recently making necessary the installation of solar-powered toilets along the trail. KENT AND DONNA DANNEN

Rosalie,'' captures the power and beauty of the highest peak in the central Front Range, a peak later renamed Mount Evans.

Much of that beauty can still be seen from Denver. In 1866, one travel writer wrote, ''in variety and harmony of form, in effect against the dark blue sky, in breadth and grandeur, I know of no external picture of the Alps that can be placed beside it.'' Fortunately, that mountain scenery inspired city founders to lay out the streets of Denver with a view of the mountains so that, as Colorado poet Thomas Hornsby Ferril puts it, every street ends ''in blue and blue, in peak and peak and sky and sky.''

The view south of Denver ends more in green. There, horizons settle into lower, more-timbered peaks known locally as the Kenosha, Tarryall, and Platte River mountains. The Tarryall Range is a twenty-five-mile ridge of low peaks running along Tarryall Creek and reaching 12,000 feet here and there. Once, the Tarryalls held one of the largest bighorn sheep herds in the West. But the Tarryall Valley is also prime habitat for developments and subdivisions, so bighorn inhabit these low hills in much smaller numbers now.

Like the Tarryalls, the Platte River Mountains and the Kenosha Range both reach into the borders of Lost Creek Wilderness, the nearest protected wilderness to Denver. Huge, weirdly shaped intrusions of granite haunt the hillsides, and Lost Creek disappears eleven times from its bed only to reappear downstream.

South of these mountains, the Front Range seems to bow low to the gods who, according to the Utes, once lived atop Pikes Peak. The Rampart Range, seen from the plains, forms a strikingly level ridge, a remnant of the same ancient erosional episode which created the flat topography around Trail Ridge Road in Rocky Mountain National Park and many of the high tablelands in the Front Range. Both the Pike and Long expeditions viewed Pikes Peak from this flat ridge. A fire lookout station once sat near Devils

Head, a huge granitic formation near the northern part of the ridge, and today the Rampart Range Road skirts the crest offering extensive views of the plains and Pikes Peak.

With the landscape bowing around it, Pikes Peak seems to poke through the sky. Although thirty peaks in the state are taller, no peak in Colorado has the vertical relief of Pikes Peak—6,600 feet from base to summit. Its summit marks a spectacular end to the Front Range, a range appropriately known as "the people's mountains."

Over two million people a year visit the Front Range in Rocky Mountain National Park, while another 350,000 people stand atop Pikes Peak. Many more thousands drive up the highest paved highway in the U.S., leading to the summit of Mount Evans. The Front Range knows both worlds and late at night, while some peaks go as

silent as the moon, the lights of more than two million people below other peaks shimmer, just like sparks from fireworks on New Year's Eve.

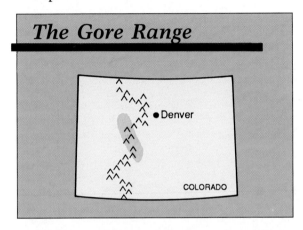

The Gore Range

High Point: Mount Powell (13,575 feet).
Other Major Peaks: Eagles Nest Mountain (13,432 feet), Jacque Peak (13,205 feet).
Cities: Vail, Silverthorne, Frisco, Kremling, Copper Mountain.
Counties: Routt, Grand, Eagle, Summit.
Public Lands: White River and Arapaho national forests, Eagles Nest Wilderness Area.

The collections of the Colorado State Historical Society contain a rusted tin can and a century-old slip of paper as yellowed and brittle as a moth's dried wings. Scribbled on the paper, taken from a mountaintop in the Gore Range, are the

Sunset silhouettes the rugged ridges of Eagle's Nest Wilderness, transforming the Gore Range into reflections of light and shadow.
BRUCE BENEDICT/THE STOCK BROKER

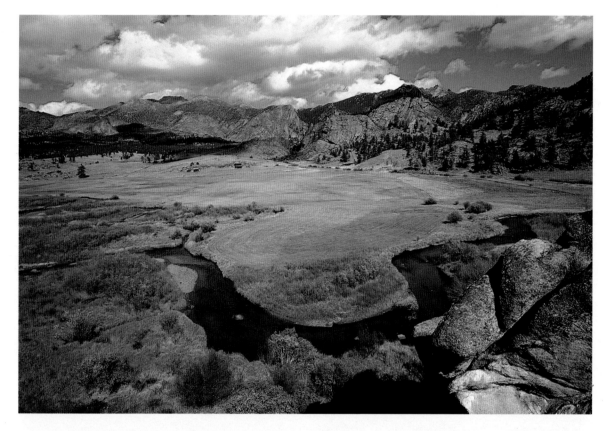

Tarryall Creek meanders below the Lost Creek Wilderness Area in the Tarryall Mountains of the Front Range, left. The Tarryalls, just west of Denver, offer some of the closest mountain recreation to the population centers along the Front Range. STEWART M. GREEN

Winter comes hard and stays long in the Gore Range, right. The Gores are pock-marked with glacial evidence—deep cirques, steep-walled cliffs, and sharp summits. Snowfields survive long into summer. BRUCE BENEDICT/THE STOCK BROKER

Major John Wesley Powell brought the range its first positive national attention. The story of his climb appeared on the front page of the October 4, 1868 edition of the Chicago *Tribune*. From the summit, Powell and O.G. Howland looked northwest to a ribbon of light that was their next path: the Colorado River leading to the Grand Canyon. Powell would return a national hero from that trip. Howland would be killed by Indians.

Gore Pass sits in the northern section of the range which begins just south of Rabbit Ears Pass and runs south seventy miles to Tenmile Gorge, a spectacular cut in the earth carved by a glacier more than a thousand feet thick. For a dozen miles south of Gore Pass, the hills are low and rolling. The Colorado River has cut another deep gash in the range at Gore Canyon west of Kremling. Then roads stop, wildness begins, and the peaks of the Gore Range dominate the skyline.

The Gore Range is rugged country. With little mineral potential, miners stayed out. With terrain that can wear the legs off a mule, many trappers stayed away. Passes in most of the range are high, rocky, and difficult, while valleys are deep, narrow, and often guarded by sharp cirques and headwalls.

As late as 1946, only one maintained trail

names of the first climbers of that mountain, including the signature of Major John Wesley Powell. From that same mountain, now known as Mount Powell, the Gore Range still looks as wild as it did on that day in 1868 when Powell and his men stood here.

The Gore Range still seems as wild as it was in 1855, too, when Jim Bridger led an Irish nobleman on an incredible hunting safari. Sir Saint George Gore, the eighth Baronet of Manor Gore, traveled in a lavishly furnished wagon complete with a portable bathtub and a "wine celler." Rising promptly at 10 a.m., Gore and Bridger combed the countryside until dark for game, employing forty men to beat the bushes and drive game in front of Gore's rifle.

Gore shot a bloody swath across North Dakota, Montana, Wyoming, and in 1855 the Gore Range of Colorado. The nobleman's gun downed an estimated two thousand buffalo, sixteen hundred deer and elk, one hundred bear, and countless smaller game like spruce grouse and rabbits. Returning to his wagon train each night after the hunt, Gore sat by lamplight reading Shakespeare aloud to Bridger. A brass plaque at the summit of Gore Pass commemorates the event.

threaded the Gore Range, a rugged cut so dangerous that two horses were killed during its construction. Even Hayden, who had seen the most rugged country in the West, called the main crest of the Gore Range a "mass of sharp-pointed peaks, crests and obelisks."

Only an hour's drive from the population centers of the Front Range, the Gore Range nevertheless remains a mystery. Many of the range's major peaks remain unnamed, or are named with letters like Peak C, a 13,150-foot spire not climbed until 1932. The Eagles Nest Wilderness which straddles the crest of the Gore Range was one of the first Colorado wilderness areas.

Now a long, winding trail snakes through fifty miles of the range on the east. In the southern spur of the range which contains Jacque Peak, Interstate 70 and Vail Ski Resort attract civilization. Early plans for Interstate 70 called for routing the highway through the heart of the Gore Range over Red Buffalo Pass, but the work of conservation leaders like Clifton Merritt succeeded in re-routing the road through Vail Pass.

A century has passed since Powell stood at the summit of the Gore Range, more than a century since Gore's rifle echoed in the canyons, and still the Gore Range looks untouched, as if a single breeze could erase even the footprints and turn back the clock.

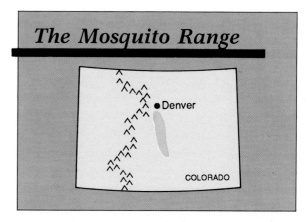

The Mosquito Range

High Point: Mount Lincoln (14,286 feet).
Other Major Peaks: Mount Democrat (14,148 feet),
  Mount Bross (14,172 feet), Mount Sherman (14,036 feet).
Cities: Fairplay, Alma, Leadville, Buena Vista.
Counties: Park, Lake, Chaffee.
Public Lands: Pike National Forest,
  San Isabel National Forest.

Typical of "faulted anticline" mountains, the peaks of the Gore Range rise abruptly from the valley floor. Although no peak in the Gore Range reaches 14,000 feet, much of the rugged range is above timberline. Mt. Powell at 13,575 feet is the range's tallest peak, first climbed by Major John W. Powell in 1868.
BRUCE W. HILL

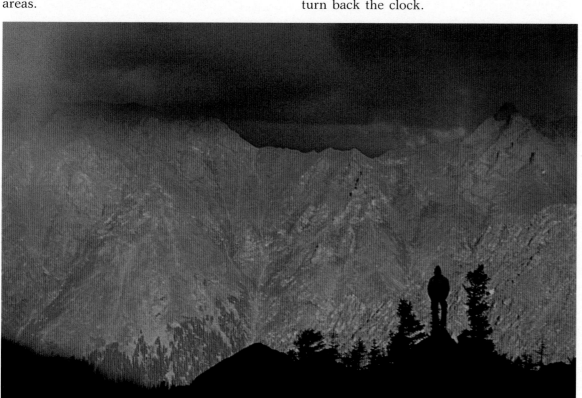

Rugged peaks can be deceptive. The Noku Crags in the Never Summer Range and Mount Zirkel of the Park Range seem to scrape the belly of the sky with sharp spires, yet neither is higher than 13,000 feet. Lone Cone rises majestically from the San Miguels with all the grace and power of a major peak, yet it is only 12,613 feet high.

The Mosquito Range rolls quietly along the western border of South Park, its summit ridge building as lazily and slowly as summer clouds. Yet, for nearly twenty miles from North Star Mountain to Weston Pass, the crest of the Mosquito Range never dips below timberline. In the stretch of high country which defines this range, from Hoosier Pass in the north to Trout Creek Pass thirty-five miles to the south, four peaks top 14,000 feet and five others climb within 300 feet of that magic number.

Such deception can be deadly. During the boom days in Leadville, 13,182-foot Mosquito Pass was a major and treacherous route to the ore fields. Strings of prospectors, too eager to wait for winter to release the pass making travel safe, died of exposure while crossing the Mosquito Range, turning what they hoped would be the route to fame and fortune into the "Highway of Frozen Death."

The Mosquito Range has one of the longest and most colorful mining histories in Colorado. Above Alma, in Buckskin Gulch, three strange circles called "arrastes" have been worn deep in the gravels of a creekbed where the mules of sixteenth-century Spanish miners turned endless circles powering a grinding wheel.

In the 1860s, disgruntled miners too late to stake claims in the Tarryalls founded a city they called Fairplay in the shadows of the Mosquito Range. Here they found both gold and silver. The diggings were good, but the deceptive heights of mountains made working them difficult. The Last Chance Mine was built at 12,600 feet on a saddle between Mount Sherman and Mount Sheridan, and the Montezuma Mine opened just a hundred

feet below the summit of Mount Lincoln.

Avalanches, deep snows that buried mining huts, cold as hard as steel, treacherous mountain trails, and an unstable market for ores made scraping a living out of the Mosquito Range difficult. Sometimes the price of ore was the least of miners' troubles. In Buckskin Joe, a mining town south of Mount Bross, a woman known only as "Silverheels" danced away the troubles of miners at local saloons. Miners came from every hill and valley to watch and forget for a while the sweat and shovels of gold mining. They came every night until 1861 when a deadly bout of smallpox ravaged the town. Men died faster than they could be buried. Mining ceased because men were afraid to go into the mines where the highly contagious disease spread quickly.

All the women and children in Buckskin Joe fled to Denver, except for Silverheels. She moved from cabin to cabin through the almost-deserted town caring for the ill, feeding them, bathing them, nursing the whole town until the sickness passed

In gratitude for what Silverheels had done, the town took up a collection and raised $5,000 for her. But Silverheels was nowhere to be found. Legend says she contracted the disease herself and it disfigured her once-beautiful face, causing her to flee in shame. With no one to give the money to, the town honored the dancehall nurse in another way, naming a peak not far from town Mount Silverheels.

Several times in the years following the smallpox epidemic, residents reported a woman with her face shrouded by a veil walking among graves in the tiny cemetery. Whenever she was approached, they said, she fled, with clicking steps as if she wore heels made of silver.

Miners were probably first to climb most peaks in the Mosquito Range and give them names. There was a strong patriotic bent among them, and peaks wear the names of political figures—Bross, for the Lieutenant Governor of Illinois; Lincoln and Sherman, for a U.S. president and vice presi-

dent, respectively. When Mount Lincoln, thought at the time to be the highest in the state, was named, miners in the area sent President Lincoln a gold bar worth $800 made of ore collected in the mines. One of the president's last official acts before his assassination was to send thanks to the miners in the Mosquito Range.

The same rough-cut roads and trails which brought miners to work now make the mountains of the Mosquito Range among the most accessible high peaks in the state. Many summits in the range can be scaled without ropes. From many of those summits, the saw-toothed peaks of the Sawatch Range are blue in the west. In the face of such views, the Mosquito Range often seems soft and easy—until the wind blows. In the Mosquito Range, looks can be deceiving, but the bite

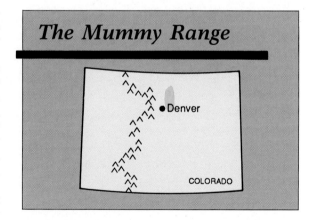

The Mummy Range

High Point: Hagues Peak (13,560 feet).
Other Major Peaks: Mount Ypsilon (13,514),
*   Mount Chapin (13,454), Mummy Mountain (13,424).*
Cities: Estes Park.
Counties: Larimer.
Public Land: Rocky Mountain National Park, Roosevelt National Forest, Commanche Peaks Wilderness Area.

The Mummy Range is viewed by millions of people each year from Trail Ridge Road and Horseshoe Park in Rock Mountain National Park.

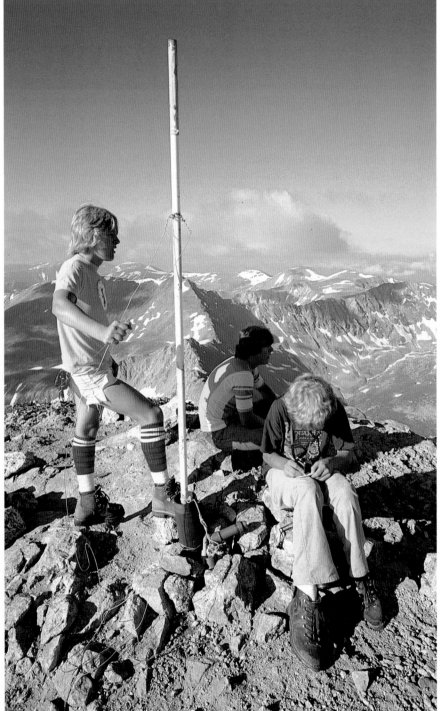

Its high peaks are visible from the highway near Cameron Pass. Even from Front Range highways, the tips of its snow-covered summits are sometimes recognizable. Yet distant highways are as close as many people get to the mountains of the Mummy Range.

The Mummy Range, for the most part, is worshipped from afar. Since the southern part of this twenty-mile spur of the Front Range lies within Rocky Mountain National Park, no roads lead into the shadows of these peaks. To reach Mount Fairchild, for example, which sits in the center of the Mummy Range, requires a twenty-mile hike from the park and then a climb of more than 5,000 vertical feet. The northern section of the range lies within Roosevelt National Forest and the Comanche Peaks Wilderness Area. While a few rough, axle-busting backroads stagger near the range, most end several miles from the peaks. The

Early mining activity webbed the Mosquito Range with old roads and trails like this one near Independence Pass, far left, now used chiefly by hikers in summer and cross-country skiers in winter. MACON COWLES

The rolling profiles of peaks like Mount Democrat make the Mosquito Range a popular family climbing range, left. Such summits were also visited by miners who combed the area in the late 1800s. Prospecting holes are commonly found far above timberline in the Mosquito Range, signs of both hard work and faded dreams. STEWART M. GREEN

Mummy Range stands alone.

Viewing the Mummy Range from afar is the best way to understand its unusual name. The skyline resembles a mummy on its back. Hagues Peak, highest in the range and fourth-highest in Rocky Mountain National Park, forms the mummy's head; Mount Fairchild is the drawn-up knees; Mount Ypsilon shapes the feet; and Mount Chapin and Mount Chiquita are the mummy's footstools. To see the resemblance takes a good imagination and just the right light.

To reach the heart of the Mummy Range takes less imagination and more boot leather. At Flint Pass, chips of stone were left behind by ancient mountain people chiseling projectile points. Centuries later, the Mummy Range was a favorite backcountry destination of Roger Toll, superintendent of Rocky Mountain National Park from 1921 to 1929. Active in the Colorado Mountain Club, Toll worked to preserve and promote the Mummy Range. In the last year of his tenure at the park, Congress, at the urging of Toll and others, extended the northern boundary of the park between Mummy Pass and Fall Mountain, thus encompassing the crest of the Mummy Range.

Toll moved on to other parks, but his touch remains on the Colorado Rockies. When he was killed in an automobile accident, Colorado erected a memorial and mountain indicator on the summit of Sundance Mountain. Many peaks identified by that indicator were climbed by Toll and many more still bear the names he suggested while a member of the Colorado Geographic Board.

The Mummy Range, although not particularly high, was chiseled by ice. To Arapaho Indians, these peaks were "White Owls," named for the many pure white snowfields dotting the mountainsides like molted feathers. Israel Rowe, on a hunt for bears in the spring of 1880, discovered that one of these snowfields was actually a glacier—the same glacier "discovered" a few

years later by William Hallett, who tumbled into a crevasse on its face. The glacier was originally named after Hallet, but the name was confusing since there is a Hallet Peak far from the glacier, and so it was eventually changed to Rowe Glacier.

Rowe Glacier has melted now into little more than a snowball on the southeast side of Rowe Peak. Though the glacier and others like it in the Mummy Range are all but gone, they left their marks. The west side of the Mummy Range is rounded and smooth. The east side, however, where wind-blown snows for thousands of years collected into glaciers, is pock-marked with cirques. Frozen water in glaciers has an almost explosive power, exerting a pressure of up to 30,000 pounds per square inch, and the east face of the Mummy Range was scarred and sculpted by the battle of such ice against rock.

Deep cirques and glaring snowfields, the ice-carved "Y" on Mount Ypsilon which gives it its Greek name, and deep valley shadows all give the Mummy Range a distinctive character—even from afar.

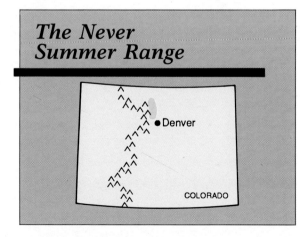

The Never Summer Range

High Point: Mount Richthofen (12,940 feet).
Other Major Peaks: Mount Howard (12,810 feet),
*   Mount Cirrus (12,797 feet), Mount Nimbus (12,706 feet),*
Nokhu Crags (12,485 feet).

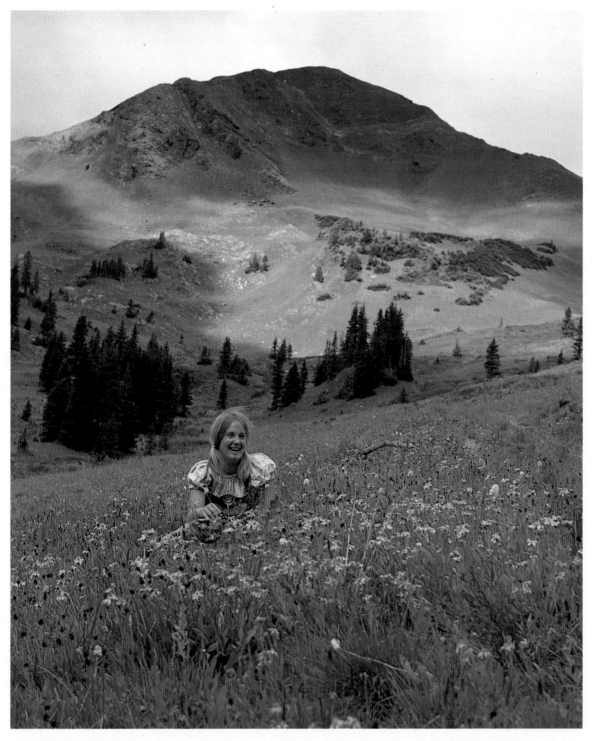

Cities: Grand Lake.
Counties: Grand.
Public Lands: Rocky Mountain National Park, Never Summers Wilderness, Arapaho and Routt national forests.

In other ranges, snow is already sloughing off high peaks like winter fat, leaving dark, triangular scars. In the Never Summer Range, however, springtime still holds shadows the color of ice. To the Arapaho Indians, these mountains were known as ''Ni-chebe-chii,'' the place of No Never Summer. White men shortened the name to the Never Summers.

The Never Summer Range stretches for ten miles from Cameron Pass to Bowan Mountain. From Mount Richthofen south, the summits carry two important lines. The first line is man-made. Roll a boulder west off any of the peaks which form the crest of the range and it will roll onto national forest land. Roll a boulder east off any of those peaks it will roll onto lands administered by Rocky Mountain National Park. The Never Summer Range forms the western horizon for much of the park. Never Summer peaks are visible from Fall River Pass and the western arm of Trail Ridge Road.

When the 1915 boundaries were drawn for what would become the tenth national park, the lines ignored topography and the Never Summer Range. Later, as those boundaries were redrawn to protect ecosystems, the border followed the summits of the Never Summers. But this left the western flanks of the range outside of Rocky Mountain National Park, exposed. Lumbering companies made large clearcuts in the range

On the western border of Rocky Mountain National Park, the Never Summer Range is one of the most popular ranges in the state. This hiking trail over Thunder Pass follows an old route to Lulu City, a town which boomed in 1879 following a gold strike nearby but was deserted only a few years later. KENT AND DONNA DANNEN

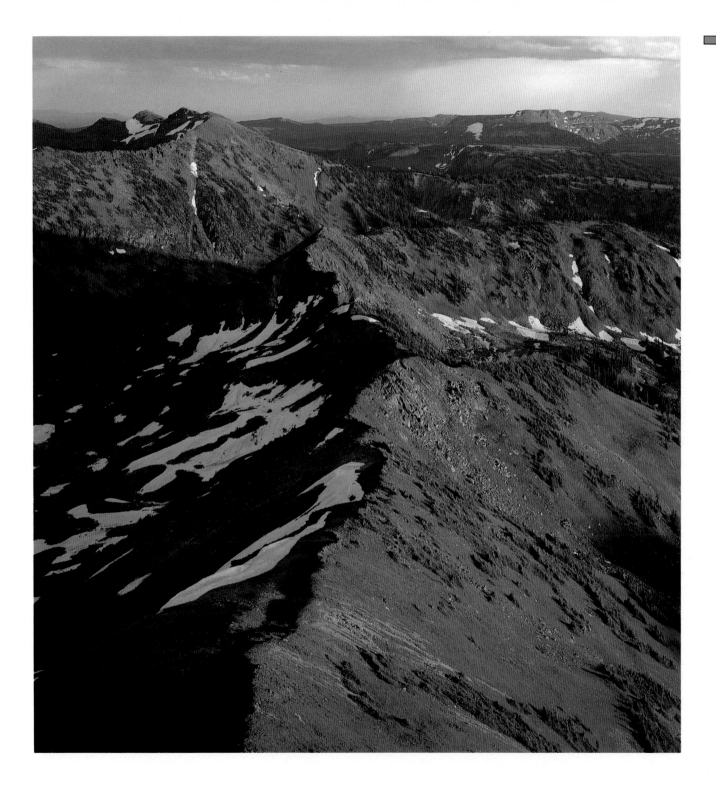

The Continental Divide arches through the Mount Zirkel Wilderness in the Park Range, forcing snow drifts only yards apart to feed waters flowing thousands of miles in opposite directions. CARR CLIFTON

The northern Never Summer Range, including the American Lakes area shown here, is under the management of the Colorado State Forest Service. Much of the eastern part of the range has been added to Rocky Mountain National Park and is managed by the National Park Service. Western areas of the range are under the jurisdiction of the U.S. Forest Service. Each agency acts under different mandates, with different management plans, and so concerted efforts to protect the Never Summers are often difficult. JOHN R. BOEHMKE

to the sky. Indians came to Red Mountain for red clays to use as war paint. Lead Mountain is so full of the metal that trappers told of using unworked stones for bullets. Iron Mountain contains so much iron that it makes compass needles go wild. Nokhu Crags is derived from the Indian word "Neaha-Noxhu," meaning Eagle's Nest.

More than names separate these peaks from the rest of the mountains in Rocky Mountain National Park. Unlike most of the park, only one trail reaches into the Never Summers, from the east up Baker Gulch in a long, winding, rocky path.

The Never Summers are darker, harder-looking. The range was not folded and faulted like the Mummy or Front ranges, but was born of fire. Rising as much as 3,000 feet from the valley floor, the peaks of the Never Summers were a small localized center of volcanic activity which scorched ranges like the Rabbit Ears and the Flattops to the west. Heat made these mountains harder, less prone to erosion and the work of glaciers, and so left them with smoother, more graceful lines.

Some scientists believe that the earth is entering another Ice Age and that it is enjoying a short springtime before another long winter. If another long, deep winter does come, perhaps it will come from here, from the Never Summers, where winter has never really disappeared.

until a 1980 act of Congress drew another boundary around 14,100 acres, creating the Never Summers Wilderness.

The second important line following the Never Summer Range is a natural one. The Continental Divide follows the crest of the range from Baker Pass to Thunder Mountain, where it makes an oxbow and heads south through the center of Rocky Mountain National Park. The headwaters of the North Fork of the Colorado River, a river which flows west into the Pacific Ocean, are situated within this oxbow loop of the Divide, giving the impression that the headwaters are east of the magic line. And rivers which flow east through the North Platte into the Atlantic Ocean seem to originate west of the nation's backbone.

Such tangled topography creates beautiful scenery, with drainages nearly criss-crossing and rains seemingly confused about where to fall. The weather which brews over these peaks inspired their names, given by James Grafton Rogers, a founder of the Colorado Mountain Club and member of the Colorado Geographic Board. These are the cloud peaks—Nimbus, Stratus, Cumulus, and Cirrus.

Not all names in the Never Summer Range refer

The Park Range

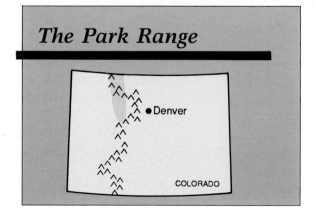

High Point: Mount Zirkel (12,220 feet).
Other Major Peaks: Big Agnes (12,059 feet),
  Mount Ethel (11,924 feet).
Cities: Steamboat Springs.
Counties: Routt, Jackson.
Public Land: Routt National Forest, Mount Zirkel Wilderness.

In spring, the Park Range seems to pulse, more water than rock. The range is veined with creeks like the Roaring Fork, Wolverine, and Mad that come alive with the thaw, tumbling down mountainsides. Ribbons of water in the north part of the range converge on Encampment Meadows where the wild Encampment River begins its long journey northeast towards the North Platte. The western part of the Park Range lies on the opposite side of the Divide and there, streams like the South Fork, Bear Canyon, and Wolverine wind together into the waters of the Elk River, which flows west to join the Yampa. Along streambanks throughout the range, beaver have gnawed and felled aspen. Among rocks in midstream, a short whistle and flash of blue means the water ouzel.

High lakes in the Park Range wake up to summer more slowly, opening like deep blue eyes as they melt. The range is speckled with high lakes—Lake of the Crags, Mica, Bighorn, Luna, and so many tiny, unnamed ponds and tarns that from the air they look like blue stars in a mountain sky.

The Park Range flows into spring, throwing off the cold and opening like a wildflower. The sound of rushing water is a constant low hum almost everywhere and the surface of almost every lake is rippled by rising trout.

The lakes and streams which tie the Park Range together are a product of glaciers which once lay deep here. The long, rolling uplands of the range

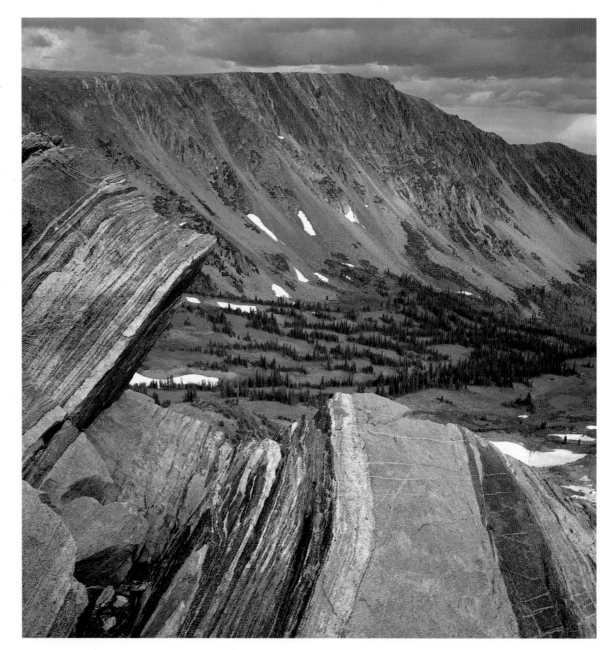

Flattop Mountain is part of the 140,972-acre Mount Zirkel Wilderness Area in the Park Range. CARR CLIFTON

were buried in Pleistocene ice caps from which scraggly fingers of glacial ice poked far down into valleys below. In the flats of the Yampa Valley to the west, large boulders called erratics were carried by glaciers and deposited in the middle of nowhere as the ice retreated.

Lake beds were scooped out by ice. Streams were cut deeper by the rush of water when ice melted. Perennial snowfields still cling to the higher slopes of the range, remnants of the recent Little Ice Age and reminders that water, as much as lines on a map, defines the Park Range.

There is rock here as well. Stretching thirty-five miles from the Wyoming border to Rabbit Ears Pass, the Park Range is a classic faulted anticline forming the western border of North Park. Much like the Front and Sangre de Cristo ranges, a sharp and dramatic fault slices the western edge of the Park Range into plunging cliffs. Most of the range is low, rising only 10,000-12,000 feet, but those inconspicuous summits carry the Continental Divide into Colorado.

Not far south into the range, however, a change occurs. Mount Zirkel is anything but inconspicuous. Its sides look rough-cut out of black ice. Though it stands only 12,180 feet tall, it is a powerful peak which rips strands from storm-clouds and weaves its own weather. Often, when the sun shines over the rest of the Park Range, dark clouds hover like buzzards over the summit of Mount Zirkel. A pamphlet of the Forest Service boasted in 1917 that ''its rocky pinnacle has never yet been scaled.'' The first recorded climb, according to William Bueler's history of Colorado climbing, was in the summer of 1936, long after most other Colorado peaks had already been bagged.

The peak's name honors petrologist Ferdinand Zirkel, who accompanied the King Survey on its exploration of the 40th Parallel. Petrology is the science of identification and classification of rock types. Zirkel found much to study here, in the mixture of granite, schist, and greenstone which makes up the crest of Park Range, formed by the Zirkel-Big Agnes-Sawtooth Uplift, and in the sedimentary formation of the more-rounded mountains surrounding it.

At one time, all the mountains stretching from the Wyoming border to Trout Creek Pass near Buena Vista were considered the ''Park Range,'' since they form the western border of South, Middle, and North parks. Today, that string of mountains is divided into the Park, Gore, Tenmile, and Mosquito ranges. The Park Range was also known as the ''Snowy Range'' for a time, because the same snows which feed creeks and lakes also pile deeply along its western flanks.

Those deep snows caused the mining tragedy at Hahns Peak, a low summit of only 10,839 feet located well west of the main range. In 1864, Joseph Hahn discovered color in his pan from creeks at the base of the peak. Generous to a fault, Hahn let two other men share in the strike and started a town nearby in the fall. Hahn and the two men volunteered to wait out the winter. One of the men left in October to bring supplies for the long stay. He never returned.

As winter tightened its grip on the Park Range, Hahn and the other man were caught in snow as deep as the treetops and ice as hard as iron. Their supplies and their hopes of a rescue party dwindled together. They could kill no game in the deep snow and slowly, cruelly, the two men began to starve.

The two almost survived winter until a spring snowstorm buried them even deeper. In desperation, they set out on foot, floundering in the new snow. Not far from the peak, Hahn could go no farther and after carrying him as far as he could, the other man left him in the snow to die. A search party reached the cabin two days later. But it was two days too late for Joseph Hahn, whose name remains on the peak.

As the search party returned to civilization with the sad tale, the mountains were already beginning to pulse with springtime. Snows were melting, and a sound familiar in the Park Range hung in the air like mist—the sound of running water.

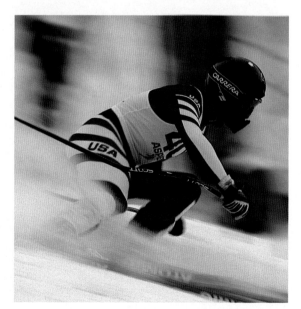

Colorado's excellent powder and steep, challenging slopes have made the state a popular stop for many world-class skiing competitions. Professional and amateur skiers from around the world, such as this U.S. Ski Team member racing on the World Cup circuit in Aspen, come to Colorado's slopes to compete in events like downhill, slalom, and even ballet skiing. DOUG LEE.

Of light and form

A thumb-sized rubbing stone carried off a summit, snapshots from Trail Ridge Road, a petroglyph etching of a jagged skyline carved in rock. For thousands of years, humans have ached to hold the mountains in their hands, to come to grips with the immensity of power, rock, light and form that is a mountain.

Humans chipped the likeness of Longs Peak into a rock below an overhang. Early artists like Thomas Moran and Albert Bierstadt revealed the mountains to the world. The tradition continues today.

Alfred Wands is a fisherman. Working the streams in Rocky Mountain National Park, his line arcing like a strand of golden light, he once rounded a bend to see Mount Ypsilon in the Mummy Range suddenly glistening in sunlight. It was a fleeting moment. But Alfred Wands, a well-known and respected landscape artist, quickly traded his rod for a paint brush and captured the moment on canvas.

That painting now hangs in the Administration Building of Rocky Mountain National Park. Wands has been painting the mountains of Colorado since he and his wife moved to Denver in 1930. Now he paints from his studio in Estes Park, with Longs Peak visible from his window.

Works by Alfred Wands have won forty-seven exhibition awards and are in the permanent collections of major museums across the country. He paints every day, usually in the field where "it is all right there in front of me, the mountains, the light, the trees." Yet his work is not a mirror image of the mountains. Wands adds the "human element," composing the subject by adding trees or creeks. The final product is more than a picture of a mountain. It is mountains seen through the eyes of an artist —an artist and a fisherman.

Robert Wands, the son of Alfred Wands, is also a landscape artist. Robert extends his vision into the cloudscape, striving to paint "the impact of how the sky and the land come together." His paintings are more interpretative. The skies play roles as powerful as the rock, and lines are graceful and powerful. His are the mountains of the mind as much as of the land.

The work of Robert Wands has also won many awards. One of the most pleasing was a faculty award from the Cleveland Institute of Art, an award his father won thirty years earlier. Both artists look at the mountains and see different forms and light, different visions. But they equally continue a tradition which began when men first carried smooth, charmed stones off of summits, trying to hold the mountains of Colorado in their hands.

Top: Painting by Robert Wands. Courtesy of Robert Wands.

Bottom: Painting by Alfred Wands. Courtesy of Rocky Mountain National Park.

The Rabbit Ears Range

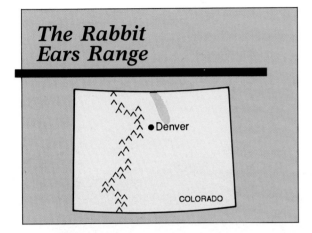

High Point: Parkview Mountain (12,296 feet).
Other Major Peaks: Rabbit Ears Peak (10,654 feet).
Cities: None.
Counties: Grand, Jackson.
Public Land: Routt and Arapaho national forests.

Some mountain ranges stand alone, like the Sangre de Cristos. Other ranges, like the Ruby Range in the Elk Mountains, are swallowed up and lost in a sea of peaks. The Rabbit Ears in northern Colorado is another type of range, more like a high-country land bridge.

The Rabbit Ears Range runs east-west for thirty miles, carrying the Continental Divide and connecting the southern tip of the Park Range with Rocky Mountain National Park at the Never Summer Range. The Rabbit Ears Range, like the Flattops and Never Summers, was a center for volcanic activity in northern Colorado during Tertiary times. Eroded volcanic formations and signs of violent volcanic activity are everywhere. Whiteley Mountain in the southwestern part of the range is finely etched with small cracks known as "columnar jointing," caused by uneven cooling of molten rock which left polygonal patterns on the face of the mountain.

Dikes, looking like the long dorsal fins of prehistoric creatures, radiate outward from the Rabbit Ears Range. These long, thin spurs were formed when magma flowed down the mountainside and cooled in vertical joints in the bedrock.

The premier volcanic formation in the range is Rabbit Ears Peak. Standing over the extreme western portion of the range, Rabbit Ears Peak is the eroded remnant of a volcanic plug where lava once reached the surface and cooled into hard rock. The softer rock around the plug eroded, leaving the Rabbit Ears standing more than a hundred feet above its surroundings and giving a name to a range, a peak, and a mountain pass. The name was first used by the Hayden Survey Party, which mapped and explored much of the West. The tall, thin "ears" of Rabbit Ears Peak are best viewed from the southeast.

One of few Colorado mountain ranges running east and west, the Rabbit Ears Range forms a bridge of another kind, too. Its crest forms the border between North Park and Middle Park. Utes used routes up Willow Creek Pass to cross between hunting grounds in North Park, which they knew as the "Bull Pen" for its herds of bull elk and buffalo, and the hunting and fishing in Middle Park near Grand Lake.

Arapaho and Cheyenne used the passes, too, and conflicts arose. One Ute legend tells of a time long before the white man came, when a large group of Utes emerged from the mountains and camped at Grand Lake in Middle Park to hunt and fish. Late at night, when tents were quiet and campfires burned low, hundreds of Arapaho and Cheyenne attacked the camp. Ute warriors put their women and children on a large raft and floated it out to the middle of the lake, to keep them safe. The battle raged for hours while, unseen by those fighting, a strong wind capsized the raft in the cold waters, drowning the women and children. Today when mists rise from Grand Lake on a cold morning, it is said to be the lost souls of those women and children searching for shore.

Muddy Pass west of Willow Creek is the lowest pass over the Continental Divide in Colorado. Only 8,772 feet at its crest, the pass proved early a dependable route even in bad weather. Fremont and his men used Muddy Pass on the triumphant return of his 1844 expedition from California. At that time, the pass was a dividing line between warring tribes and a party of Arapaho Indians in Middle Park told Fremont they considered "all whom they met on the western side of the mountains to be their enemies."

Indian wars are long past and vast herds of buffalo are gone. Yet, on some passes and summits in the Rabbit Ears Range, horizons still bridge those same distances felt by Fremont and the mountain men who looked down into both North and Middle parks.

The Rawahs

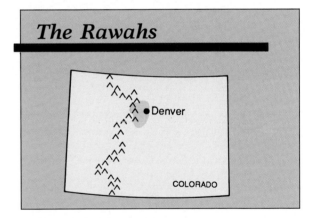

High Point: Clark Peak (12,951 feet).
Other Major Peaks: Sickle Mountain (12,654 feet),
  South Rawah (12,644 feet), North Rawah (12,473 feet).
Cities: Glindive
Counties: Larimer, Jackson.
Public Land: Colorado State Forest, Roosevelt National
  Forest, Rawah Wilderness Area.

Distinct and unmistakable for miles, the spires of Rabbit Ears Peak have served as a landmark for travelers in north-central Colorado for centuries.
JEFF GNASS

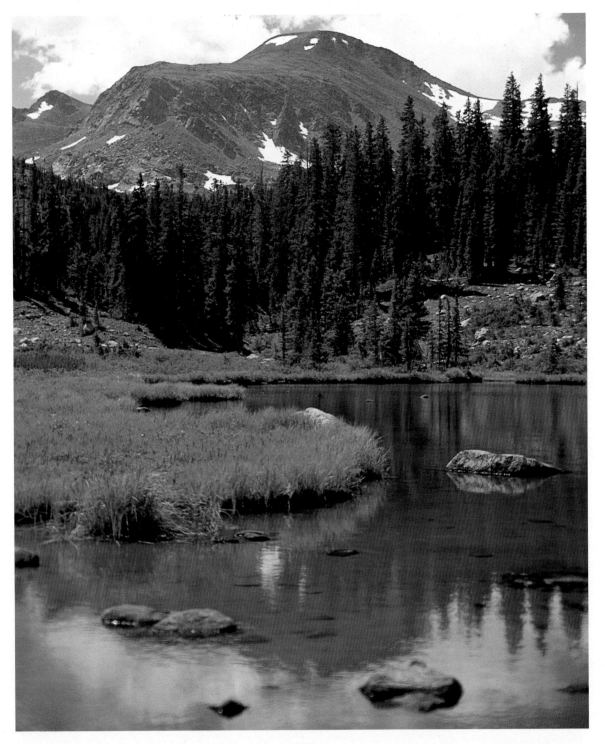

Indians understood the silence they heard in these mountains and the power they saw in these peaks. Rawah, they called it—"wilderness." The United States Congress also called it wilderness passing a bill adding 75,000 acres of the Rawahs, comprising most of the eastern flank of the range, to the National Wilderness Preservation System.

The Rawahs in Colorado are an extension of Wyoming's Medicine Bow Mountains. On many maps, the name extends south with the range, a name derived from a legend of Indians gathering in these mountains to make bows out of wood given "good medicine" by the gods. The Colorado portion of the range, the Rawahs, runs from Wyoming border to Cameron Pass in a ridge of 10,000- to 12,000- foot peaks. Both sides of the range feed high-country trout streams and the southern half of the eastern slope, known as the "Lake District," is dotted with lakes like Twin Crater, Island, Blue, and a string of high ponds known as the Rawah Lakes. Hiking and horseback trails lead into many parts of the range, particularly from the east, and the Medicine Bow Trail winds for forty miles across the high country of the range, often above timberline.

The western section of the range, which forms the eastern edge of North Park, makes up the 72,000-acre Colorado State Forest managed by the State Board of Land Commissioners. This twenty-eight-mile-long park, regulated much like state parks, is open to the public for hunting, camping, and fishing.

Named for an Indian word meaning "wilderness," the Rawahs, left, are also called the Medicine Bow Mountains. The range is still mostly wilderness, protected on the east by the 76,394-acre Rawah Wilderness Area and on the west by the 72,000-acre Colorado State Forest. RON S. MELLOTT

Looking east from Wilson Peak, right, the San Juans seemingly recede into an endless sea of peaks. ROBERT BASSE

Tucked into the western side of the Rawahs, where the range veers slightly, are the East Sand Hills and North Sand Hills, beautiful and dreamlike sand dunes. For thousands of years, wind has scoured across North Park and, over time, sand carried in those winds has collected in this pocket of the Rawahs.

East Sand Hills is the bigger of the two, covering approximately 640 acres of land in light yellow sand. A delicate ecosystem of plants and animals has evolved around these "cold climate dunes"

and is currently designated a Colorado Natural Area by the Department of Natural Resources.

Tens of thousands of visitors each year are attracted to the Rawahs by good fishing, alpine beauty, a fine system of trails, and the fact that the range is within easy driving distance of Front Range population centers. Many of the most-visited sites are on delicate lands that border timberline. There, a fire ring can leave charred rocks visible for thousands of years and a tree hacked for firewood may not be replaced for hun-

dreds of years. As rugged as the high country appears, it is really as fragile as wildflowers. Too much use and too little knowledge about low-impact camping techniques have scarred the wilds of the Rawahs with bare ground at over-used campsites and rutted trails.

Attempts to bring back the wildness are slow to show results, measured in lifetimes in places. Revegetation programs have been undertaken at some denuded lakeside campsites and an intensive user education effort has begun.

The Rawahs are not the only Colorado range showing signs of overuse. The Indian Peaks, Chicago Basin in the San Juans, and Maroon Bells in the Elks also suffer. Wilderness is not measured by names or even congressional designations, but by strings of elk making for a pass and by unbroken horizons, subtle threads which cannot be repaired as easily as campsites. Rawah, the Indians called it—wilderness.

The San Juans

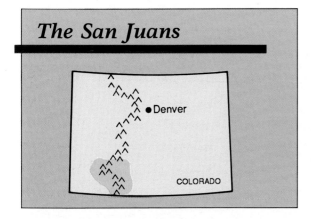

High Point: Uncompahgre Peak (14,309 feet).
Other Major Peaks: Mount Sneffels (14,150 feet),
   Windom Peak (14,087 feet), Mount Eolus (14,084 feet),
   Sunlight Peak (14,059 feet), Handies Peak (14,048 feet),
   Red Cloud Peak (14,034 feet), Wetterhorn Peak (14,015 feet),
   San Luis Peak (14,014), Sunshine Peak (14,001).
Cities: Pagosa Springs, Telluride, Silverton,
   Durango, Ouray, Lake City, Creede.
Counties: Montezuma, La Plata, Ouray, San Juan, Mineral,
   Hinsdale, Archuleta, Saguache, Rio Grande, Conejos.
Public Land: San Juan, Uncompahgre, Rio Grande, and
   Gunnison national forests; South San Juan, Weminuche, Big
   Blue, Mount Sneffels, and La Garita wilderness areas.

Dwarfed climbers stand atop Cirque Peak in the Sneffels Range, right, a jagged spur of the larger San Juans. DAVID MUENCH

The San Juans, far right, encompass more than 10,000 square miles of mountains. TOM ALGIRE

In Colorado's San Juan Mountains, horizons stack up like cordwood. After the next ridge is another, and another. At the headwaters of the Conejos, in the Weminuche country, along Twilight Creek, and in the shadow of Wolf Tooth, horizons are overwhelming and people gather at tiny campfires like moths around flames. As one early explorer put it, no other Colorado range has horizons so ripped by "skylines marvelously bold and wild." It is a mountain kingdom.

The San Juans make up the largest single range in the U.S. Rockies. They encompass more than 10,000 square miles, an area larger than the state of Vermont. The San Juan Mountains include all the mountainous terrain south from the Gunnison River, west of the San Luis Valley, and east of the Dolores River. They include at least seven mountain groups known locally as ranges—the La Plata Mountains, La Garita Mountains, Needles and West Needles, Rico Mountains, Grenadier Range, and Sneffels Range.

In all, ten of the fifty-four Colorado peaks over 14,000 feet are found in the San Juans, and twenty more of the next fifty highest. Other notable peaks don't even make that list—Three Needles overlooking Telluride; Mount Hesperus, one of the westernmost points of the range; the castle-like cliffs of Potosi Peak; and Storm King, one of the ragged edges of the Grenadiers.

Colorado's largest designated wilderness, the 405,031-acre Weminuche, is located in the heart of the San Juans. The South San Juan, Big Blue, La Garita, and Mount Sneffels wilderness areas surround the Weminuche, protecting more than 800,000 acres of the range as wilderness. Potential additions could increase that total to nearly a million acres.

A dozen rivers have headwaters in the San Juans, including the Rio Grande and San Juan as well as candidates for the Wild and Scenic Rivers System like the Piedra and Los Pinos.

Pike saw the endless horizons of the San Juans from the crest of Medano Pass in the Sangre de Cristo Range during his 1806 expedition. Fremont encountered the same constantly receding horizons on his disastrous 1848 expedition. Both were looking at the San Juans from the east across the floor of the San Luis Valley.

Moonrise over the La Plata Mountains, part of the San Juans. TOM BEAN

The San Juans are split into two parts by the Rio Grande River. South of the Rio Grande lie the peaks of the South San Juan Wilderness, wild country which can hold its secrets. In 1952, for example, near the Rio Grande Pyramid farther west, a government trapper took the "last" grizzly from the Colorado Rockies. For twenty-seven years, the mountains held their secret.

Then, on a warm and sunny September 23, 1979, Ed Wiseman, a long-time hunting guide in the San Juans, was attacked by a lone female grizzly at the headwaters of the Navajo River near Navajo Peak. With a hand-held arrow, Wiseman managed to fight off and eventually kill the bear. Tooth and skull measurements of the carcass by bear expert Tom Beck of the Colorado Division of Wildlife confirmed the first grizzly in the Colorado Rockies in more than a quarter century, hidden for all those years in the depths of the San Juan Mountains.

To the north of the Rio Grande, the La Garita Mountains were the site of Fremont's losing bout with the San Juan winter. Trees hacked off at the six-foot snow line for firewood and the tattered remains of a sled mark the fateful camps of Fremont around Mesa Mountain.

Tucked into another corner of the La Garitas are cliffs that seem to dance in spires and shadows that float like ghosts. This is the Wheeler Geologic Area, a collection of light-gray, highly eroded towers carved by erosion from volcanic ash, formations like "The City of Gnomes," "Phantom Ships," and "The White-Shrouded Ghosts." The Wheeler Expedition first ventured here, and by 1908 this was designated a natural area. Today the Wheeler Geologic Area is a candidate for wilderness designation.

Fremont had in mind the vast, roadless heart of the San Juans, now the Weminuche Wilderness, when he called the range "one of the highest, most rugged, and impracticable of all the Rocky Mountain Ranges, inaccessible to the trappers and hunters even in the summer time." Few

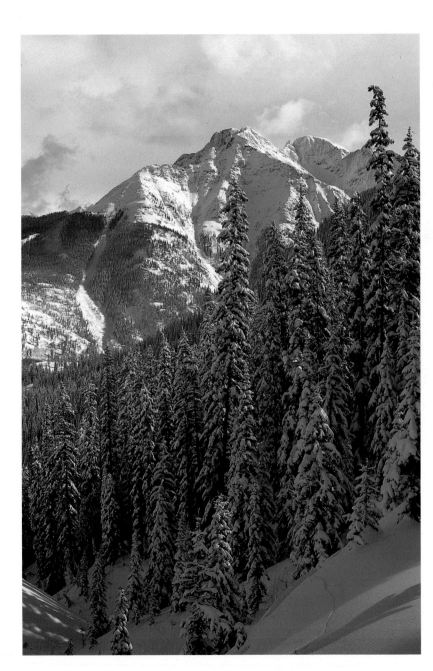

Deep snow blankets North Twilight Mountain in San Juan National Forest.
RENE PAULI

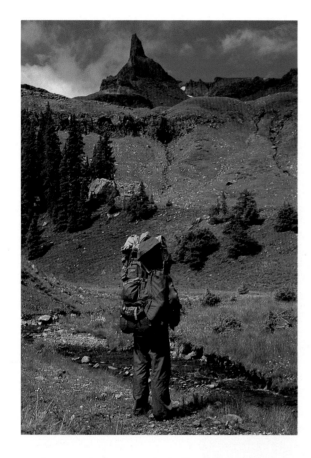

Coxcomb Peak juts from the Big Blue Wilderness near the Middle Cimarron River. LARRY ULRICH

roads, even today, penetrate the San Juans. Those that do were first laid down by the sweat and energy of one man.

Although his portrait has been etched into a stained glass window overlooking the Colorado State Senate, few can recall his name. Thousands of people enjoy the view of the Sneffels Range from the Dallas Divide, but only a handful know that one of the peaks they see bears the name of the man who opened the San Juans. He was Otto Mears, pathfinder, and the roads he blazed have become the routes of highways and railroads.

When a wagonload of his produce bound for market tipped over on a trailless pass, Mears decided to build a road. His first in the San Juans connected Saguache to Lake City in 1871, the same year gold was discovered there, and his toll road became a gold mine of its own as miners swarmed over it towards the San Juans. Next, Mears built a forty-mile road to the silver mines in Silverton and then a hundred-mile road to the growing town of Ouray.

Toll booths along his roads charged 50 cents per person and $5 per wagon. Everyone paid, even General MacKenzie and his troops as they returned from removing Utes from the San Juans in 1881. That was also the year of the Dallas Divide Road, which first brought supplies to Telluride and then began attracting tourists who come even today to view the splendor of the Sneffels Range.

By far the most famous Otto Mears undertaking was the 8.5-mile road from Ouray to Red Mountain. The path followed a ledge blasted out of the mountainside at a cost of $4,000 per mile. Later, in 1920, that stretch was expanded using gold-producing gravels for its road bed and became known as the "Million Dollar Highway," a route followed by U.S. 550 today. Every curve and every grade is a lasting tribute to Otto Mears, the Pathfinder of the San Juans.

The western edge of the San Juans, the Needles, is ragged as a torn page, shredding the skyline into stormclouds. From the top of Engineer Mountain, the men of the Hayden expedition provided the first-known written description of the Needles, saying, "...in the distance appeared a group of very scraggy mountains about which the clouds were circling, as if it were their home."

As awesome as the Needles and Grenadier ranges

appeared to the men of the Hayden Expedition, it was the Wheeler Survey which left one of the most vivid descriptions of the region. "Nowhere in Colorado," a journal-keeper wrote, "can be found such steep slopes, such shapeless crags, such rocky and impassable ravines, such generally detestable characteristics and features as are seen here." The sharp outlines of the range brought to their imaginations horrible outlines—"there the likeness of the shattered outspread wings of some gigantic bird, and again of the grim grinning teeth of Death."

A lack of mining activity combined with impassable terrain has kept the Needles isolated and alone. Three peaks in the Needles top the magic 14,000-foot line, and the range has become one of Colorado's prime climbing areas. The San Juans as a whole have spawned considerable climbing history. Much of it was made by a group of young climbers including David Lavender, T. Melvin Griffiths, Chester Price, Lewis Giesecke, Bob Ormes, Gordon Williams, Charles Kane, Ruth McClintock, Carleton Long, and others who called themselves the "San Juan Mountaineers."

Dwight Lavender, a skilled climber and leader, was the driving force behind the group. With Lavender as their leader, the San Juan Mountaineers stood atop scores of San Juan summits between 1928 and 1936. Not only did they leave scrawled names in tin can summit registers, but the group also compiled *The San Juan Mountaineers' Climbing Guide to Southwestern Colorado*, one of the first of its kind in the history of Colorado mountaineering. The book boosted the young sport of mountain climbing and opened the way for others to enjoy the challenges of the San Juan Mountains.

Much of the climbing guide was the work of Lavender, who died of poliomyelitis in 1934 at the age of twenty-three. In 1976, the United States Board of Geographic Names paid tribute to his work in the San Juans by naming a 13,160-foot peak in the La Plata mountains "Lavender Peak."

Now Dwight Lavender and the San Juan Mountaineers will remain a part of those "skylines marvelously bold and wild" that make up the horizons of the San Juan Mountains.

The San Miguel Range

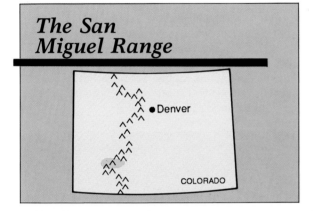

● Denver

COLORADO

High Point: Mount Wilson (14,246 feet).
Other Major Peaks: El Diente (14,159 feet),
Wilson Peak (14,017 feet), Lizard Head (13,113 feet),
Lone Cone (12,163 feet).
Cities: Telluride, Ophir.
Counties: Dolores, San Miguel.
Public Land: Uncompahgre, San Juan national forests;
Lizard Head Wilderness Area.

It takes imagination to see the lizard in the Lizard Head atop Lizard Head Peak. From the north, the peak looks as straight and true as a finger pointing skyward. From the east, it takes on the shape of a throne for a god.

The Lizard Head may be hard to recognize because it is falling apart. The famous formation sits at the eastern edge of the San Miguel Range, a northwestern offshoot of the San Juan Mountains stretching twenty miles from Lizard Head Pass to Lone Cone. The strange profile of the rock spire jutting four hundred feet from the mountain top caught the eye of men in the Hayden Survey who saw a monster's silhouette in the rock and gave it the descriptive name.

The peak became famous and often-

The snows of the San Miguel Range feed the headwaters of rivers such as the Dolores and San Miguel and sustain internationally know winter resorts such as Telluride, located nearby. TOM TILL

photographed, frequently decorating popular postcards and brochures throughout the area. Otto Mears even used an artist's rendition of the rock as the logo for his Rio Grande Northwestern Railroad. With all this publicity, the public was shocked by reports in 1912 that the Lizard Head had fallen off.

The reports turned out to be a hoax, and the Lizard Head is not likely to come crashing down anytime soon. Yet, there are occasional reports of large pieces caking off, and the peak *is* slowly crumbling. Formed from soft conglomerates and volcanic tuffs, rock which is brittle and easily eroded, the cliffs of Lizard Head Peak are made up of what climbers call "garbage rock." Handholds break off under pressure, cracks won't hold hardware, and rocks fall from above to make the Lizard Head at only 13,113 feet "the most difficult summit to reach in Colorado," according to a recent article in *Climb* magazine.

An older article, in *Outing* magazine, 1921, details the adventurous tale of its first successful climb. Albert Ellingwood and Barton Hoag scaled the western side of the formation, feeling the mountain crumbling under their fingertips. "Ab-

solutely the whole surface of the rock is loose and pebbles rain from its sides as readily as needles from an aging Christmas tree," wrote Ellingwood. Rock slides in "small avalanches" rumbled like thunder as the two climbed. Highly skilled in climbing techniques, the two climbers made the summit safely but in a longer time than they had expected. Forced to come off the mountain in the dark, Ellingwood tied a lantern to a long rope and strung it along as the two climbed back down by its faint yellow glow.

While the Lizard Head sheds its skin like a snake, other peaks in the San Miguel Range are as hard as tempered steel. Out of nowhere as Colorado Highway 145 tops a rise outside of Telluride, the Mount Wilson group rises like a steel gate on the southern horizon, creating a view familiar to generations of travelers. Even in the late 1800s, the elite of Telluride, then a booming mining town, drove carriages out to "Society Curve" for picnics beneath Mount Wilson and its neighbors.

The view is impressive. A low, glaciated valley dips to its knees in front of the peaks—Mount Wilson and Wilson Peak, both over 14,000 feet;

A mountain sketchbook / 108

Dolores Peak (13,290), and Sunshine Mountain (12,930). Many higher peaks in the San Miguels rose as "nunataks," summits which stuck through the glacial ice.

To the west, where the Colorado Rockies meet mesa country, the San Juans rarely rise above 11,000 feet. But before the mountains surrender completely to flat horizons, Lone Cone rises like a crescendo. Only 12,613 feet high, Lone Cone is one of the most beautiful and symmetrical mountains in the Rockies. Its contours are almost sensual in their sweep to the summit. Standing as isolated as a lightning rod, Lone Cone is a weather-maker, attracting dark clouds and storms while the air around it shivers with the sparks of lightning bolts. This is where the mountains lie down, the westernmost major peak in the Colorado mountains.

The Sangre de Cristo Range

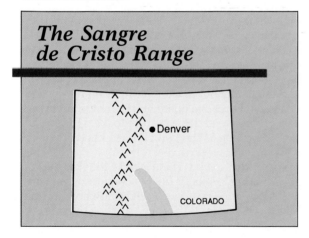

The 14,191-foot Crestone Needle in the Sangre de Cristo Mountains is one of Colorado's classic climbs. Its summit was the last of the 14'ers to be conquered, first climbed in 1916 by Albert Ellingwood and Eleanor Davis. ROBERT BASSE

High Point: Blanca Peak (14,345 feet).
Other Major Peaks: Crestone·Peak (14,294 feet), Crestone Needle (14,191 feet), Kit Carson Mountain (14,165 feet), Humboldt Peak (14,064 feet), Mount Lindsey (14,042 feet), Little Bear Peak (14,037 feet).
Cities: Crestone, Westcliffe.
Counties: Fremont, Saguache, Custer, Alamosa, Huerfano.
Public Land: San Isabel, Rio Grande national forests; Great Sand Dunes National Monument.

The winds blowing across the San Luis Valley slap the Sangre de Cristo Range with cold so sharp that the air tastes of iron and the creeks freeze solid to the bottom. Along Medano Creek flowing out of the heart of the Sangre de Cristos, the

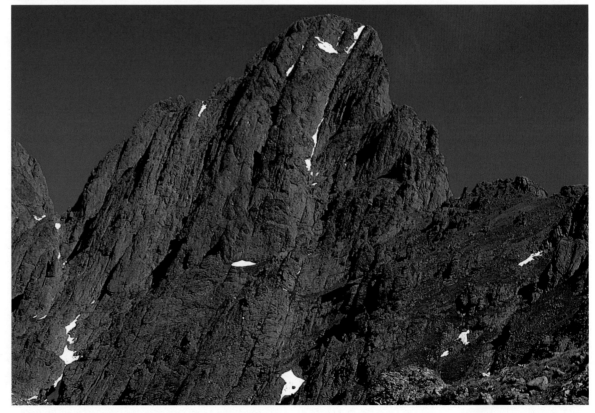

trunks of trees look hacked with blaze marks. Slabs of stripped bark as big as a man's chest have been ripped from the ponderosa pines. There is debate as to when—the 1830s? the 1860s?—but a hard cold had trapped an Indian tribe wintering along the creek and in desperation they turned to the trees. They ate bark and may have fed it to animals or even used it as protection against the wind. Today the scarred trees, being considered for listing on the National Historic Register, stand as living artifacts, their pitch-stained wounds testimony to the hard winters of the Sangre de Cristo Range.

The Sangre de Cristos form a classic mountain range, curling like an ocean wave out of the lowlands. Peaks, sharp and blue as smoked glass against the morning sky, catch fire from the setting sun and bleed with the deep red color of alpine glow which inspired their name, "the Blood of Christ." From the Arkansas River on the north to La Veta Pass on the south, the Sangre de Cristos form a picket fence of 13,000-foot summits along the eastern edge of the San Luis Valley, the wind whistling through passes as if through slats.

Although it is in places only twenty miles wide, no highways cross the range. Medano, Music, and Mosca passes provide the main routes for horsepackers and hikers and have been known and traveled for centuries. When Pike crossed Medano Pass in the depths of winter, he followed a well-worn trail and blaze marks cut by Indians who had used the route for untold years to reach hunting grounds in the San Luis Valley. Kit Carson, who may have had a cabin near the Crestone group and whose name remains on the fourth-highest peak in the range, led Fremont and his men over Music Pass and down Sand Creek. Not far from there, in the 1940s, a team from the Colorado Museum of Natural History discovered a cave strewn with artifacts of the Aztecs believed to have been stolen and hidden by Spaniards centuries ago.

In two places, the Sangre de Cristos rise above 14,000 feet. Over Willow and Spanish creeks, the summits of the Crestone group look as sharp as chipped arrowheads. Humboldt Peak was climbed early, at least by 1883, but the higher three—Kit Carson Peak, Crestone Peak, and the Crestone Needle—stood unclimbed until 1916, longer than any 14,000-foot peaks in Colorado.

At its southern tip, the range changes, gets darker, harder, and higher. The peaks of the Sierra Blanca are huge blocks of Precambrian granite thrust up by localized uplift to form the 14,000-foot summits of Little Bear, Mount Lindsey—also called Old Baldy—and Blanca peaks.

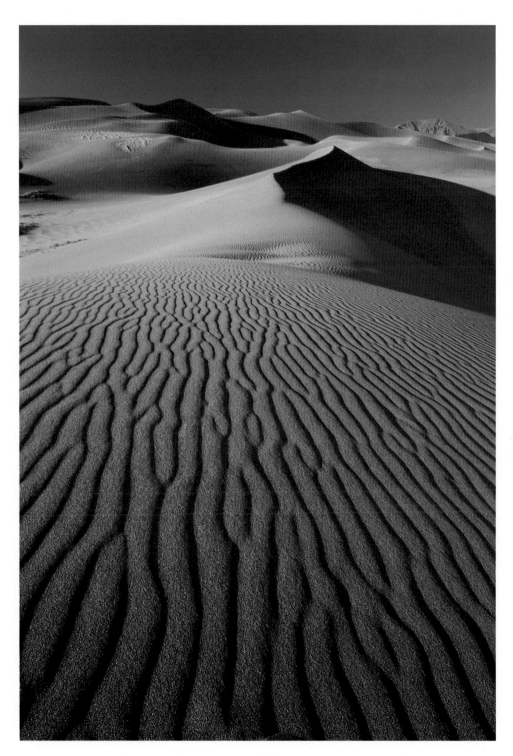

Winds ripple the surface of sand dunes in the Great Sand Dunes National Monument. Infinite combinations of predominantly westerly winds, reverse winds, and eddies create a variety of sand dune types.
GAIL DOHRMANN

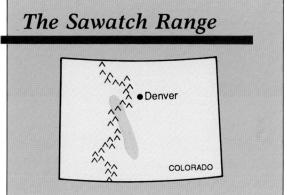

The Sawatch Range

High Point: Mount Elbert (14,433 feet).
Other Major Peaks: Mount Massive (14,421 feet), Mount Harvard (14,420 feet), La Plata Peak (14,336 feet), Mount Antero (14,269 feet), Mount Shavano (14,229 feet), Mount Princeton (14,197 feet), Mount Belford (14,197 feet), Mount Yale (14,196 feet), Tabeguache Mountain (14,155 feet), Mount Oxford (14,153 feet), Mount Columbia (14,073), Missouri Mountain (14,067 feet), Huron Peak (14,005 feet), Mount of the Holy Cross (14,005 feet).
Cities: Garfield, Buena Vista, Twin Lakes, Malta.
Counties: Lake, Chaffee, Pitkin.
Public Land: White River and San Isabel national forests; Holy Cross, Mount Massive, Collegiate Peaks and Hunter Fryingpan wilderness areas.

For all of their high peaks and inaccessible ridges, the Sangre de Cristos have a heart of sand. Near the center of the range where it trends slightly to the south, the Great Sand Dunes National Monument collects sand from winds blowing off the San Juans and slamming against the peaks of the Sangre de Cristos. Through thousands of years, winds have created a range of dunes six miles across and reaching as high as seven hundred feet.

The dunes are constantly dancing with the wind, shifting as if restless and alive. With a switch in the winds, the dunes creep slowly towards a forest and, grain by grain, entomb its trees until another whim of the winds begins just as slowly to uncover "ghost forests" of silver-gray stumps. Creeks flowing strong out of the mountains vanish in the sands. Grasses ebb and flow like tides at the edges of dunes. In the dark, when the night is still, the dunes sometimes emit a humming sound like distant singing, the music of shifting sands.

The lonely echoes of valleys, creeks like threads of silver light, unbroken chain of high peaks, and shifting ecosystem of sand dunes have all made the Sangre de Cristos a rare opportunity for Colorado. Nowhere else in the 2.6 million acres of designated wilderness in the state is a whole mountain range protected. A proposal to create a 265,000-acre Sangre de Cristo Wilderness stretching from Hayden Pass to Mount Blanca offer that opportunity. The proposal has the support of conservation groups throughout the state but seems stalled in Congress. This opportunity won't last forever. Wilderness is a fragile resource and in the shifting winds of politics, this chance to protect the Sangre de Cristos may be as fleeting as deer tracks in sand dunes.

The Sawatch Range is made up of mountains fit for people. When the annual Mountain Life Festival is underway in Buena Vista, notes as clear as mountain ice ring from a handmade dulcimer. A storyteller describes a log cabin deep in the mountains that the sun never shines on it. A woodworker with a handmade pipe smokes what smells like pine bark and chisels on a wooden mountain. The setting is perfect.

The Sawatch Range contains fifteen of the state's fifty-four peaks over 14,000 feet, including four of the five highest—Mount Elbert, Mount Massive, and Mount Harvard, which rank first, second, and third, respectively; and La Plata Peak, which ranks fifth behind Mount Blanca in the Sangre de Cristo Range. The Sawatch Range runs nearly a hundred miles from the Eagle River to Monarch Pass, reaching forty miles wide in places. Still, many of the highest peaks can be scaled by walking.

To the Indians, these mountains were Saguache or ''waters of the blue earth,'' named for the springs around Mount Princeton and the lake which once sat in the San Luis Valley. The name was a tongue-twister. As one miner put it, the only way to pronounce it was to sneeze it. So the spelling was changed to reflect the sound of the word: Sawatch.

Whether they could pronounce its name or not, the miners came to this range, spreading out from rich finds in places like California Gulch east of Leadville to find other valuable ores. Dozens of mining towns such as Independence, Massive City, Ruby, and Everett sprang up, wild towns

As a winter sun sets, left, snow as dry as sand transforms the Great Sand Dunes National Monument. Even now, however, the stillness of the dunes is an illusion—winter winds and spring snowmelt ensure that the dunes are continually shifting. STEPHEN TRIMBLE

On the morning of August 24, 1873, the men of the Hayden Survey Photographic Unit led by photographer William Henry Jackson stood atop Notch Mountain to photograph a legendary cross of snow on nearby Mount of the Holy Cross, above. The photographs Jackson took that day made the 14,005-foot Sawatch mountain famous throughout the world and were displayed at Centennial Celebrations in 1876. Poet Henry Wadsworth Longfellow wrote of ''a mountain in the distant West/that sun-defying, in its deep ravines/displays a cross of snow upon its side.''

By 1929, the area around Mount of the Holy Cross was declared a National Monument and thousands of people were making the pilgrimage. In the 1950s the area was included within White River National Forest, where today it is the centerpiece of 126,000-acre Holy Cross Wilderness. WARREN MARTIN HERN

with as many bar stools as miners and more dance halls than mess halls. Mines were located high above timberline on the peaks of the Sawatch, and so it is likely that most summits in the range were reached early by miners. But it was a mountain which they probably did not climb that brought the first worldwide acclaim to the range.

In 1873, William Henry Jackson led the Hayden Survey Photographic Unit in search of the Mount of the Holy Cross. For years stories had circulated of a peak that bore a snowy cross on its face, but when Hayden and Jackson visited the Sawatch Range in the summer of that year, they could find no one who had seen the cross with their own

eyes. After a long, difficult climb in which their mules played out below timberline and 120 pounds of photographic gear had to be carried by hand, clouds obscured their view. They spent the night in a wet, cold camp.

On the morning of August 23, 1873, though, the skies cleared and Jackson took one of the most famous mountain photographs in history. The legends were true. The cross, 1500 feet high and 750 feet across, is on the northeast face of Mount of the Holy Cross, the northernmost 14,000-foot peak in the Sawatch Range. The sight of the cross through Jackson's photography and later through the artwork of Thomas Moran and the poetry of

Henry Wadsworth Longfellow stirred the nation and the world. The summit of Notch Mountain from which the cross is best viewed became a pilgrimage. One Denver pastor, with the help of forest rangers, carried more than two thousand handkerchiefs belonging to people from around the world to be blessed in the waters of The Bowl of Tears lake below the cross. One woman, bed-ridden for eight years, was carried up the trail to view the cross and reportedly was "cured."

Such sights and stories attracted the eyes of the world to the Sawatch Range. The mountain was designated a National Monument in 1929, but in 1950 that designation was rescinded. Today, the cross overlooks the 126,000-acre Mount of the Holy Cross Wilderness Area, and the path to the vantage point on Notch Mountain is still worn by the feet of hikers.

Mount of the Holy Cross has been included and excluded and included again on Colorado's list of 14,000-foot peaks. The last official elevation reading admitted it to the group with just five feet to spare. Grizzly Peak just south of Independence Pass, the highest crossing of the Continental Divide in Colorado, was not so lucky. Considered a 14,000-footer until 1965, it is now officially listed at 13,988 feet.

Ironically, many of the most rugged peaks in the range—Ice Mountain, Mount Etna, Grizzly Peak, the Three Apostles—are under 14,000 feet. The

The southern end of the Sangre de Cristo Range is dramatically marked by 14,338-foot Blanca Peak, the pillar of what is known locally as the Sierra Blanca Massif. Much of this section of the range was a part of major land grants awarded to early settlers. Today, with several 14'ers in the area including Blanca, the Crestone Needle, and Crestone Peak, the Sierra Blanca Massif is a focal point for recreation in the long, thin Sangre de Cristo Range. DAVID MUENCH

tallest peaks, clustered in a group around Mount Elbert, seem less formidable. In fact, Mount Elbert, named for Colorado's second territorial governor, Samuel Elbert, is one of the few high peaks anywhere in the state which can be climbed easi-ly on skis in winter.

From the western windows of Buena Vista, a section of the Sawatch Range known as the Col-legiate Peaks dominates the skyline. J.D. Whitney, whose name graces the highest peak in the con-tinental U.S., Mount Whitney in California, began naming Sawatch peaks for colleges on an 1869 survey of the peaks. Whitney was head of the first graduating class of the Harvard School of Mining when he brought graduates to the Sawatch Range, and in honor of the school, the highest peak became Mount Harvard. The second highest was named Mount Yale, after Whitney's alma mater. The others—Princeton, Columbia, and Oxford— were named later in keeping with the theme.

The Collegiate Peaks are tall, bulging from the Arkansas Valley more like muscles than cut glass. On autumn weekends when artists and musicians gather in the valley to celebrate mountain life, the peaks create the perfect backdrop, with streaks of gold in the aspens and new snow dusting the sum-mits. The musicians play and the woodcarver carves, celebrating life in the mountains.

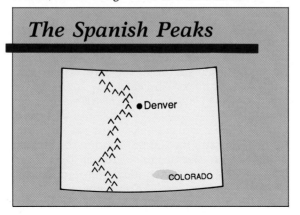

The Spanish Peaks

High Point: East Spanish Peak (12,683 feet).
Other Major Peaks: West Spanish Peak (12,262 feet).
Cities: Cuchara, Gulnare.
Counties: Huerfano, Las Animas.
Public Lands: San Isabel National Forest.

The Spanish Peaks look guarded. Long, sharp blades of rock called "dikes" radiate from the mountains. Geologists have identified more than four hundred dikes jutting from the peaks like knife blades, some for fourteen miles. The dikes formed when fissures in the earth were filled with molten magma spewing from the craters of East and West Spanish Peaks. Slowly, the magma cool-ed into steel-hard rock and after thousands of years the softer, encasing rock wore away, leaving the Devil's Stairway, Profile Rock, Sawtooth Rock, and hundreds of other dikes to stand guard.

According to Indian legend, East and West Spanish Peaks suckled the earth. "Huajatolla," they called the twin peaks—Breasts of the Earth. Under skies as blue as lake water and wrapped in a quilt of thick timber, the Spanish Peaks look like the paradise legend says once existed here. They rise not from other mountains but 6,000 feet straight from the plains, two of the easternmost mountains in the state. The rich volcanic soil which surrounds the peaks has spawned fertile farmlands irrigated by the snows which melt off the mountainsides.

According to Indian legend, no one in the shadows of these peaks would die and any dream of a person sleeping near the mountain would come true. Once, too, there was gold on these mountains, used for offerings to the gods who lived there. Then three Spanish priests arrived. Two tried to bring religion to the Indians, but the third schemed to plunder the gold. First, he forc-ed Indians to mine the sacred gold. Then he kill-ed them and started for Mexico. Somewhere along the route he disappeared and never made it to Mexico. Years later, in 1811, large nuggets of gold were found far out on the southern plains many miles from any possible natural source.

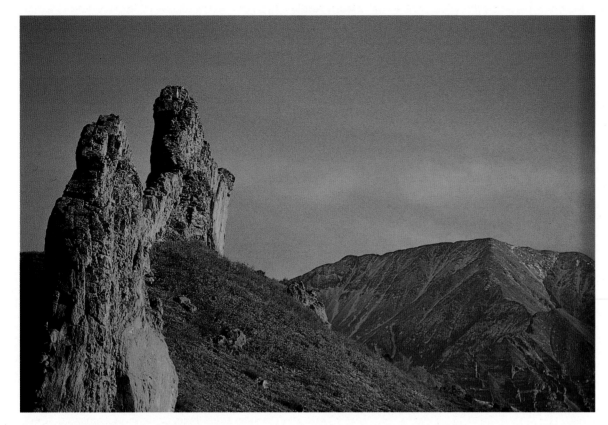

This volcanic dike at West Spanish Peak and the Cucharas River Canyon testifies to the fiery origins of the Spanish Peaks. JACK OLSON

The Tenmile Range

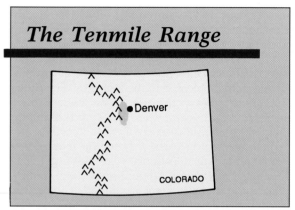

High Point: Quandary Peak (14,265 feet).
Other Major Peaks: Fletcher Mountain (13,951 feet), Pacific Peak (13,950 feet), Wheeler Peak (13,690 feet).
Cities: Breckenridge, Copper Mountain, Frisco.
Counties: Summit.
Public Lands: Arapaho National Forest.

Like many mountains which rise steeply above their surroundings, the Spanish Peaks stir up the weather. Stormclouds gather so frequently on these peaks that Indians believed the summits were home to the rain gods and that a rocky crag on the south side of West Spanish Peak was the birthplace of clouds. The rain keeps the farmland around the peaks lush and productive. In Walsenburg, thirty miles to the east, a festival known as the Spanish Peaks Fiesta is held each year to celebrate harvest.

Just half an hour from Walsenburg and an hour from Trinidad, the Spanish Peaks nourish the wilderness. As the cities of the Front Range continue to grow in population and area, nearby mountain areas become more and more important as recreation spots, wildlife and flora

habitat, and wilderness resources. The Spanish Peaks offer wilderness trout fishing for cutthroat, rainbow, and brook trout in miles of creeks feeding into the Apishapa River to the south and the Cucharas River to the north. Elk venture into the valleys, and rocky cliffs hide mountain lion. Currently designated a 19,600-acre Wilderness Study Area, the Spanish Peaks may someday be included in the National Wilderness Preservation System.

In 1977 the Spanish Peaks were added to the National Registry for Natural Landmarks. But as the first of the Rockies to cut the horizon from the southeast, they have long been landmarks drawing travelers into the mountains. This is where the mountains start. This is the beginning of paradise.

The mining boom throughout the Colorado Rockies had little impact on the Tenmile Range. A few prospectors who came too late or weren't lucky enough to get in on the action elsewhere ended up at a small town perched near the crest or "climax" of Fremont Pass. A town called Fremont Pass was born. One of those men was Charles Senter, and he made a small strike involving a strange gray rock.

By 1900 the gray rock was identified as molybdenum, but there was little use for it at the time. Other ores played out, and the town nearly followed. Then World War I came along, and the city renamed Climax boomed.

Molybdenum is used as an alloy to strengthen metal in weapons. When the war hit, the Defense Department turned to Bartlett Mountain, the mountain of molybdenum, in the Tenmile Range. The reddish mountain just outside of town was sitting on perhaps the world's largest deposit of the strategic metal, and now there was a use for it. By the 1930s the boom was full-blown, and in

1938 over $20 million of the ''gray gold'' had been produced.

Like most mining economies, of course, molybdenum has had its booms and busts. In 1958, a low cycle silenced the mine. Then, in 1969, more than $105 million in ore was taken out of the mountain. In the 1980s, a depressed market has quieted the mine again. Such economic swings have brought prosperity and poverty to cities near the Tenmile Range.

The huge ''glory hole'' where Bartlett Mountain has collapsed recalls better days in the range. The long sludge-filled tailing ponds stretching in nearby valleys recall the worst days. Today, the mine operates at only partial capacity. Large layoffs in the early 1980s stunned Climax, and only now have a few miners resumed work. For a time, at least, silence has returned to these mountains.

The Tenmile Range sounds simple. It sits between the Gore and Mosquito ranges, providing a bridge for the ridge of peaks between the northern Park Range and the southern end of South Park. To the north, the Tenmile Range is bounded by Tenmile Creek near Frisco. To the south, it runs as far as Hoosier Pass.

Despite its name, the Tenmile Range is twelve miles long. These peaks were the stomping grounds of miners who knew what walking felt like. To them, the hike from the confluence of Tenmile Creek and the Blue River to the early mining town of Breckenridge felt like about ten miles. So naturally the mountains they crossed on that hike became the Tenmile Range.

Geologists call the wedge-shaped Tenmile Range an ''asymmetrical anticline.'' From the east the slopes are gentle, rising quietly to a ridge of numbered peaks like Peak One, Peak Seven, and Peak Ten that reach 12,000-13,000 feet. Even taller mountains like Quandary Peak, tallest in the range, slope easily on the eastern side. In fact Quandary Peak, like Mount Elbert in the Sawatch Range, can be scaled on skis—via the gentle eastern slope.

But the western edge of the Tenmile Range has been severely faulted, forming steep cliff faces. From the west, Pacific Peak resembles the Matterhorn and the wedged cliffs of Quandary Peak's west face give the mountain a dramatic look that belies its easy route from the east.

Quandary Peak is the only 14,000-foot peak in the Tenmile Range. Its shape makes it popular with skiers and hikers. It owes its intriguing name to shiny rocks on its flanks. In the 1860s, when miners were leaving no stone unturned in their search for riches, they found an ore on this mountain that they had never seen before. Even in Breckenridge, experts in geology could not identify the ore. Everyone was in a quandary and the name stuck on the mountain like late-summer snowfields. Today, geologists still don't know what the strange ore is.

Breckenridge, where many ores of that time were brought for identification or as proof of a claim, was one of few early mining camps to survive the turbulent gold rush era. It served as a supply depot for many outlying towns that vanished with the ore. Today, another noise

Crystal Peak, 13,852 feet, guards the distant waters of the Wheeler Lakes area in the Tenmile Range. Abundant lakes and streams, including Tenmile Creek and the Blue River, at the base of the mountains make this range home to some of the best trout fishing in the state. MACON COWLES

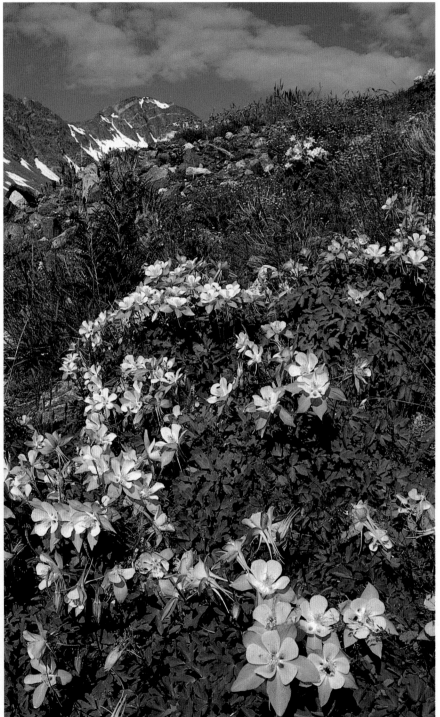

comes from the mountains near Breckenridge—not the sound of mountains being mined, but the sound of skiers. The ski slopes at Breckenridge, descending from the Tenmile Range, are among the best in the nation. The snow is "champagne powder," deep and light. Along the main street, many storefronts preserve the character of mining days and wooden sidewalks still echo with footsteps of gunslingers. But those days are gone. On this side of the Tenmile Range the gold is as white and cold and thick as a Christmas snowstorm.

The Wet Mountains

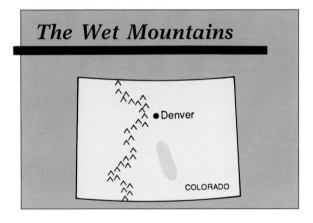

A field of elephant head grows on Boreas Pass, far left, a route once used extensively by miners on the route to Breckenridge. Clustered upturned flowers along leafy stems resemble an elephant's trunk—hence the plant's name—but the unusual shape of the flower also facilitates pollination and reduces the chance of hybridization with other species. JAMES FRANK

The Tenmile Range rises out of the valley of the Blue River, left. Watered by the river and by highcountry creeks which cascade into it, hillsides such as this one in Monte Cristo Gulch explode with blooming columbine each summer. STEWART M. GREEN

High Point: Greenhorn Peak (12,349 feet).
Other Major Peaks: St. Charles Peak (11,789 feet), Wixson Mountain (11,121 feet), Adobe Peak (10,188 feet), Badito Cone (8,942 feet).
Cities: Wetmore, Williamsburg, Beulah, Rye.
Counties: Fremont, Custer, Pueblo, Huerfano.
Public Land: San Isabel National Forest.

From the window of a small plane flying the ridge of the Rocky Mountain Front as it slices the plains of Colorado, the Wet Mountains look like a tentative brush stroke on an artist's canvas. The range forms a deep green ridge rising hesitantly out of the plains to join the Rocky Mountains. From the sky and even on a relief map, the Wet Mountains look less like the beginning of mountains than the end of plains. They are on the edge.

Structurally, the Wet Mountains are the last wisp of the Front Range anticline. Cloaked in green timber, the ridge of 9,000- 12,000-foot peaks trends southeast from its head near Horseshoe Mountain and along the Arkansas River, diverging for twenty-five miles before it reaches its southern terminus fifty miles south at Badito Cone along the Huerfano River. In its ores and in its large eastern faultline, where black Precambrian core rocks shove through younger sedimentary formations, the Wet Mountains mirror in miniature the large Front Range to the north.

Still, the Wet Mountains have a personality of their own, split between mountains and plains, reflected in the names of features—Badito Cone, the volcanic vent at the end of the range; Hardscrabble Creek; Dry Creek Canyon; Middle Muddy Creek; Scraggy Peaks; Round Top Mountain; and Antelope Mountain.

From St. Charles Peak, both worlds unfold. To the east, the plains are wide and lonesome. To the west, the snowy summits of the Sangre de Cristo Range loom across the Wet Mountain Valley. Snows that collect in the Wet Mountains feed small streams and tumble in waterfalls like Apache Falls. State roads like Highway 165 and Highway 92 follow low passes through the Wet Mountains,

and Forest Service roads web the lowlands.

One area in the Wet Mountains remains untouched—the 22,300-acre Greenhorn Mountain Wilderness Study Area. There, from the flanks of Greenhorn Mountain to the tip of Badito Cone, roads and most trails stop. The Santanna and the Bartlett trails lead into this wild terrain where the above-timberline summit of Greenhorn Mountain overlooks deep canyons like Gomez and Red canyons.

Greenhorn Mountain is shrouded with legend. A Comanche war chief called Cuerno Verde or "greenhorn" by his many enemies was as violent as a rutting bull elk with its horns still in velvet or "green." His arrogant claims to own the Wet Mountains aggravated General Anza, governor of New Mexico. In 1779, on the flanks of Greenhorn Mountain, the two forces battled and the Indian warrior fell. The mountain where he died now bears his name and the Wet Mountains are sometimes known locally as the Cuerno Verdes.

Another battle almost a hundred years later led to the first recorded climb of Greenhorn Mountain. On Christmas Day, 1854, Indians raided a settlement along the Arkansas known as Pueblo. Five hundred volunteers combed the nearby mountains for the raiders, and a skirmish along the Apishapa River led them between the Spanish Peaks and Wet Mountains. Looking for a strategic scouting location, one group of men under Colonel St. Vrain climbed "the Horn."

Indians were driven out of the Wet Mountains early, but their echoes remain. Early Indian campsites are hidden in canyons, preserved on windy buttes, and scattered along Forest Service roads that today lead to modern campsites. Standing at such primitive sites, it is easy to imagine a gentle evening wind, the hushed flutter of birds' wings, and a lone hunter looking east over the horizons of the plains, or west into the dark silhouette of the Sangre de Cristo Range, or down at his campfire in these mountains that sit between.

The Williams Fork Mountains

High Point: Coon Hill (12,757 feet).
Other Major Peaks: Ptarmigan Peak (12,480 feet),
    Ute Peak (12,298 feet).
Cities: Silverthorne, Kremling.
Counties: Summit, Grand.
Public Land: Arapaho National Forest.

Like a stealthy trapper, the mountain range named for Ol' Bill Williams sneaks through Colorado just north of the Blue River. For most of its route, it keeps low, under the cover of timber. Near the eastern edge where the Williams Fork Mountains butt up against the Continental Divide, they blend into the Front Range as convincingly as an elk against a brown autumn hillside. This range gets little notice, tucked quietly between the Divide and the high peaks of the Gore Range across the Blue River. The highest peak in the Williams Fork Mountains is hard to pick out even among the lower peaks that surround it. The Williams Fork Mountains are easy to miss. Ol' Bill would have liked it that way.

William Shirley Williams was a tall drink of water, wiry as an old mule, and tough as saddle leather. The "old" part of the name worn by "Ol' Bill Williams M.T." had little or nothing to do with his age. The name was bestowed as an honor on all the most respected mountain men: Jim "Ol'

Gabe" Bridger, "Ol' Broken Hand" Fitzpatrick. The "M.T." in Williams' name was purely of his own doing. Even if he did say so himself, which he did, Williams could out-shoot, out-cuss, out-trap, out-drink, out-ride, and out-gamble any man in the mountains. Naturally, the self-inflicted initials stood for "Master Trapper."

However good he was at trapping beaver to make money, though, Williams was twice as good at spending it. Once, he came out of the mountains with $6,000 worth of pelts to trade at Bent's Fort along the Arkansas River. Before the money even warmed in his hand, he bought several wooden kegs full of Taos Lightning and cracked them open with his axe, inviting everyone within earshot to help themselves. By the time the spree was over, Williams had to sign a promissory note just to buy the "possibles" of beans and gunpowder to get him through another year in the mountains.

He rode slumped like a half-empty sack of potatoes. But he rode nearly every valley and side creek in the Rockies. In the few short years of the mountain man era, he became famous among his peers as one of the best. When the last rendezvous broke up, he became a well-respected and sought-after guide.

Whether Fremont or Williams misled the 1848 Fremont expedition up a creek fifteen miles short of the intended route and into a fatal disaster may never be known. Although Williams was not one of the eleven men killed by the cold and starvation in camps along Embargo Creek, that tragedy proved his undoing. In spring, Williams and another man were dispatched to recover the expedition's equipment left behind in the snow. At a camp during that mission, Utes attacked and killed Williams and his partner.

In a fitting tribute to his life in the mountains, the Utes—who said they hadn't recognized Williams by the dim firelight and didn't mean to kill the man who was married to a Ute—gave him a chief's funeral, dancing the mourning dance,

chanting the death song, and covering his grave with pine boughs.

In another, more lasting honor, Williams' name went to this mountain range. That raised some confusion. On most maps, the string of low peaks paralleling the Blue River to the north are clearly marked the Williams Fork Mountains. But on other maps, the peaks within the Hunter Fryingpan Wilderness Area northeast of Aspen are called "The Williams Mountains." And the stretch of dusty hills south of the Yampa River in northwestern Colorado take their name from one of the river's tributaries: the "Yampa Williams Fork Mountains."

Tracking down the story of how three mountain ranges in the same state came up with such similar names is more difficult than tracking a windstorm over slickrock. History sometimes leaves no tracks. That is just the way Ol' Bill Williams would have wanted it. ■

In a land enchanted

At 14,000 feet, the light is sharp and clear as morning ice because air is sliced with twice as much ultraviolet radiation and 25 per cent more light than at sea level. The sky is as blue as deep water because of a reflecting process known as "scattering" which splits light waves around particles in the air.

The high country is enchanting, strange and unwordly to visitors accustomed to tamer horizons and the safety of trees. In the high places, space is as raw and pure as the light. Humans have recognized the power of such places since the first climber sat atop a summit in a vision quest.

Colorado is mountains. Although much of eastern Colorado is strung in lines as straight as a well-made fence and much of western Colorado is dug deep in canyons, the mountains in the midsection bind the state together. Ranges dominate maps the way skylines dominate the lives of those who live here and the memories of those who only visit. No one can see a mountain and remain unchanged. The sight of a peak, even from a distance, charges the landscape—brings it alive. A mountain on the horizon becomes an anchor, the cornerstone over everything and every life within its shadow.

Mountains define Colorado. The history of the state, both human and natural, is in great measure the history of mountains. Gold scratched out of mountainsides, elk making for a pass blown free of snow by the wind, skiers carving S-turns in powder, ragged edges of timberline ablaze with morning sun, slats of ghost towns creaking like the backs of miners who came and went—the personality of Colorado is mirrored in its mountains as clearly and as beautifully as the reflection of a peak in a still pond. Colorado is mountains.

Those mountains, today, have received some protection. Colorado contains more than 23 million acres of public land, much of it studded with mountains. The U.S. Forest Service, the state's biggest landholder, manages more than 14 million acres divided into eleven national forests. Within that mountain kingdom, twenty-three sections totalling 2.6 million acres are included within the National Wilderness Preservation System, protecting parts of every major mountain range in the state. Almost.

The glaring exception is the Sangre de Cristo Range. One of the highest, wildest and most stunning collections of mountains in the West, the Sangre de Cristos have so far been overlooked for wilderness designation. The range represents a unique opportunity, for while most other wilderness areas include only small sections of ranges, proposals to create a 265,000-acre Sangre de Cristo Wilderness would protect an entire mountain range ecosystem. Those proposals, however, seem stalled within the managing agency and stymied by the political climate.

Despite the sprawling mountain lands of the Forest Service, the centerpiece of Colorado's mountains remains Rocky Mountain National Park, under the jurisdiction of the National Park Service. To the world, this *is* the Colorado Rockies and the 410 square miles of wild mountain scenery and 84 peaks above 10,000 feet represents mountains in their finest light.

Thousands of acres of other mountain ranges have been protected by other means, enough to fill the widest horizons—the Colorado State Forest wrapped around the western edge of the Rawahs; natural areas like Mount Goliath; county lands; even city lands like the Boulder Mountain Parks which encompass the Flatirons of the Front Range. Each is a recognition of the importance of mountains to the state of Colorado.

Spectacular Maroon and North Maroon peaks tower above Crater Lake in the Elk Range.
DENNIS W. JOHNS

However, boundaries are not enough. The gravest threats to Colorado's high country ignore lines on maps. Increasing emissions from automobiles, power plants, smelters, and other sources cloud once-crystal-clear vistas.

As ephemeral as the values of vistas may seem, the haze foreshadows even greater dangers to the mountains. Recent research indicates that precipitation with a pH level of less than 5.6—acid rain—has fallen on the mountains of Colorado, and that the greatest incidence of this tainted precipitation has occurred in areas above 7,500 feet, the heart of the high country.

To mountains, acid rain is death. Fragile ecosystems with thin soils lack the stability and composition to adequately buffer lakes, streams, fisheries, wildlife, and vegetation from the effects of acid rain. Damage is magnified by the inability of ecosystems to heal themselves because of short growing seasons. The same mountains which seem so untouchable and remote are like an exposed throat to the fangs of acid rain. A stronger Clean Air Act and further research on the vulnerability of the high country to acid rain are keys to coming to grips with this silent killer.

A more visible threat to Colorado's mountains comes from a less likely source. With its harsh climate and inaccessability, the high country has never been a crowded place—until now. Recent increases in the popularity of outdoor sports—hiking, climbing, camping, fishing—have disturbed silence of peaks with the echoes of Vibram-soled footsteps. Recreationists have chased much of the wild out of the Indian Peaks, parts of the Rawahs, the Chicago Basin in the San Juans, and other ranges, trampling vegetation, circling high lakes like fire pits, and tainting the water. The Colorado mountains are being "loved to death."

Stricter regulations, user education, volunteer groups which have revegetated areas, and a rethinking of the whole concept of wilderness are all beginning to resurrect the wild in these wilderness areas. Just as we loved them almost to death, we can love them back to life.

Mountains are patient. Even compared to a 150-year-old cushion plant clinging to the tundra or a 2,000-year-old bristlecone pine, the Rockies are ancient. Geologically, however, they are young, and without major glaciers or restless volcanoes to age them, the Colorado Rockies will be around a while. Man is the newcomer here, still green in the ways of living with, rather than just in, a landscape. The piled stones of game-drive systems built by the first mountain people still stand unbroken, and chipped projectile points and shards of pottery are a kind of fresh footprint of mankind in the mountains.

Attitudes are changing. Slowly the glaciers of human thought and feeling are altering the landscape of land use management. Signs of renewal are everywhere—in a ghost town brought back to life as one of the world's foremost scientific field stations; in the completion of the Colorado Trail; in the stands of towns like Crested Butte, weighing mountain life against mining profits; and in gatherings like the Mountain Life Festival in the Sawatch Range. The change comes slowly but the mountains are patient, as patient as stone. ∎

The view from 14,256-foot Long Peak above ''The Keyhole'' tempts many a climber to rest.
DENNIS W. JOHNS

Colorado's skyscrapers: the centennial peaks

Pike estimated that Pikes Peak was 18,581 feet high, which would have made it one of the highest peaks in the world. That miscalculation was just the first round in a continuing controversy over the height of Colorado's mountains. At various times, almost a dozen different peaks have been considered the "highest" in Colorado. The list of 14,000-foot peaks stood for years at 46, climbed to 53 in 1965 and since has wavered between 53 and 54 due to the dispute about Ellingwood Peak in the Sangre de Cristo Range and its right to be called a separate mountain.

The Ellingwood controversy points out the difficulties in listing the highest hundred mountains in Colorado, the state's "Centennial Peaks." What is a mountain? Separate peaks atop a single mountain—such as the four summits of Mount Massive—are sometimes given the status of individual peaks and sometimes considered only ridges of one peak. North Maroon Peak sits less than 250 feet from Maroon Peak and yet is considered a mountain of its own. The controversy has been further confused by lack of accepted criteria to define a "mountain."

One of the latest attempts to formulate a definition appeared in the June, 1985 issue of *Trail & Timberline,* the publication of the Colorado Mountain Club. To warrant individual status, the article maintained, a peak must be "perceived visually as a separate mountain from at least two directions," have its own ridge system, drop at least three hundred feet from its summit to its saddles, and be located at least one-third mile from other summits. Hedging a bit, the criteria stipulate that all those peaks considered 14,000-footers by the USGS remain on the list.

Whatever their height, Colorado possesses some of the most challenging and beautiful peaks in the world. Arguments doubtless will continue, but here is a list, based on the above criteria, of the Centennial Peaks in Colorado, the highest hundred.

Rank	Peak	Elevation	Range
1.	Mount Elbert	14,433	Sawatch
2.	Mount Massive	14,421	Sawatch
3.	Mount Harvard	14,420	Sawatch
4.	Mount Blanca	14,345	Sangre de Cristo
5.	La Plata Peak	14,336	Sawatch
6.	Uncompahgre Peak	14,309	San Juan
7.	Crestone Peak	14,294	Sangre de Cristo
8.	Mount Lincoln	14,286	Mosquito
9.	Grays Peak	14,270	Front
10.	Mount Antero	14,269	Sawatch
11.	Torreys Peak	14,265	Front
12.	Castle Peak	14,265	Elk
13.	Quandary Peak	14,265	Tenmile
14.	Mount Evans	14,264	Front
15.	Longs Peak	14,256	Front
16.	Mount Wilson	14,246	San Miguel
17.	Mount Shavano	14,229	Sawatch
18.	Mount Princeton	14,197	Sawatch
19.	Mount Belford	14,197	Sawatch
20.	Mount Yale	14,196	Sawatch
21.	Crestone Needle	14,191	Sangre de Cristo
22.	Mount Bross	14,172	Mosquito
23.	Kit Carson Peak	14,165	Sangre de Cristo
24.	El Diente Peak	14,159	San Miguel
25.	Maroon Peak	14,156	Elk
26.	Tabeguache Mountain	14,155	Sawatch
27.	Mount Oxford	14,153	Sawatch
28.	Mount Sneffels	14,150	San Juan
29.	Mount Democrat	14,148	Mosquito
30.	Capitol Peak	14,130	Elk
31.	Pikes Peak	14,110	Front
32.	Snowmass Mountain	14,092	Elk
33.	Mount Eolus	14,083	San Juan
34.	Windom Peak	14,082	San Juan
35.	Mount Columbia	14,073	Sawatch
36.	Missouri Mountain	14,067	Sawatch
37.	Humboldt Peak	14,064	Sangre de Cristo
38.	Mount Bierstadt	14,060	Front
39.	Sunlight Peak	14,059	San Juan
40.	Handies Peak	14,048	San Juan
41.	Culebra Peak	14,047	Culebra
42.	Ellingwood Peak	14,042	Sangre de Cristo
43.	Mount Lindsey	14,042	Sangre de Cristo
44.	Little Bear Peak	14,037	Sangre de Cristo
45.	Mount Sherman	14,036	Mosquito
46.	Redcloud Peak	14,034	San Juan
47.	Pyramid Peak	14,018	Elk
48.	Wilson Peak	14,017	San Miguel
49.	Wetterhorn Peak	14,017	San Juan
50.	North Maroon Peak	14,014	Elk
51.	San Luis Peak	14,014	San Juan
52.	Huron Peak	14,005	Sawatch
53.	Holy Cross	14,005	Sawatch
54.	Sunshine Peak	14,001	San Miguel
55.	Grizzly Peak	13,988	Sawatch

Stately Byers Peak, 12,804 feet, rises above lake, forest and clouds near Winter Park.
ROD WALKER/THE STOCK BROKER

Rank	Peak	Elevation	Range	Rank	Peak	Elevation	Range	Rank	Peak	Elevation	Range
56.	Stewart Peak	13,983	San Juan	71.	Emerald Peak	13,904	Sawatch	86.	Hagerman Peak	13,841	Elk
57.	Pigeon Peak	13,972	San Juan	72.	Horseshoe Mountain	13,898	Mosquito	87.	Half Peak	13,841	San Juan
58.	Mount Ouray	13,971	Sawatch	73.	Creede Peak	13,895	San Juan	88.	13,841 Peak	13,841	Tenmile
59.	Fletcher Mountain	13,958	Tenmile	74.	Vermillion Peak	13,894	San Juan	89.	Turret Peak	13,835	San Juan
60.	Ice Mountain	13,951	Sawatch	75.	13874 Peak	13,874	Sawatch	90.	13,832 Peak	13,832	San Juan
61.	Pacific Peak	13,950	Tenmile	76.	Mount Buckskin	13,865	Mosquito	91.	Columbine Peak	13,831	Sawatch
62.	Cathedral Peak	13,943	Elk	77.	Vestal Peak	13,864	San Juan	92.	Jupiter Peak	13,830	San Juan
63.	Mount Hope	13,933	Sawatch	78.	North Apostle	13,863	Sawatch	93.	13,828 Peak	13,828	Sangre de Cristo
64.	Thunder Peak	13,932	Elk	79.	Jones Mountain	13,860	San Juan	94.	Jagged Mountain	13,824	San Juan
65.	Mount Adams	13,931	Sangre de Cristo	80.	Clinton Peak	13,857	Mosquito	95.	13,823 Peak	13,823	Sawatch
66.	French Mountain	13,922	Sawatch	81.	Dyer Mountain	13,855	Mosquito	96.	Mount Silverheels	13,822	Mosquito
67.	Gladstone Peak	13,913	San Miguel	82.	Crystal Peak	13,852	Tenmile	97.	Rio Grande Pyramid	13,821	San Juan
68.	Mount Meeker	13,911	Front	83.	Mount Edwards	13,850	Front	98.	Teakettle Mountain	13,819	San Juan
69.	Casco Peak	13,908	Sawatch	84.	California Peak	13,849	Sangre de Cristo	99.	13,811 Peak	13,811	San Juan
70.	Red Mountain	13,908	Culebra	85.	Mount Oklahoma	13,845	Sawatch	100.	Dallas Peak	13,809	San Juan

The first to reach the top

PIKES PEAK (14,110)—Edwin James (Stephen Long expedition), July 14, 1820. First major peak in the United States Rockies to be climbed.

LONGS PEAK (14,256)—John W. Powell, William N. Byers, August 23, 1868.

POWELL PEAK (13,534)—John W. Powell, September 26, 1868. Highest peak in the Gore Range.

LONE EAGLE PEAK (11,920)—Carl Blaurock, Bill Ervin, Stephen Hart, September 2, 1929.

LIZARD HEAD (13,113)—Albert Ellingwood, Barton Hoag, August, 1920.

CRESTONE NEEDLE (14,191)—Albert Ellingwood, Eleanor Davis, July 24, 1916. The last 14,000-foot peak in Colorado to be climbed.

PIGEON PEAK (13,972)—William S. Cooper, John Hubbard, July 11, 1908.

JAGGED MOUNTAIN (13,824)—San Juan Mountaineers, August, 1933.

EL DIENTE (14,159)—P.W. Thomas, N.G. Douglass, September 2, 1890.

MOUNT SNEFFELS (14,150)—Hayden Survey Party, September 10, 1874.

BLANCA PEAK (14,338)—Frank Carpenter, Gilbert Thompson (Wheeler Survey Party), August 14, 1874.

PYRAMID PEAK (14,018)—Percy Hagerman, Harold Clark, August 31, 1909.

NORTH MAROON PEAK (14,014)—Percy Hagerman, Harold Clark, August 25, 1908.

RIO GRANDE PYRAMID (13,821)—Wheeler Survey Party, 1874.

ICE MOUNTAIN (13,951)—John L.J. Hart, October 4, 1931.

MOUNT EVANS (14,264)—Albert Bierstadt, 1863.

MOUNT AUDUBON (13,223)—Charles C. Parry, 1862.

ARROW PEAK (13,803)—Carelton Long, John Nelson, 1932.

MOUNT PRINCETON (14,197)—William Libbey, July 17, 1877.

COXCOMB PEAK (13,656)—Henry Buchtel, August 16, 1929.

A climber rappels 140 feet off "The Maiden" high above Boulder. JOE ARNOLD JR

A mountain of names

The mountains of Colorado stood nameless for millions of years, until humans first walked among their shadows. When Roger Toll and the Colorado Mountain Club began installing summit registers in the early 1900s, many peaks still didn't have names. A Colorado Geographic Board was appointed by the governor in May of 1915 to sort out the mountain of names. Yet even today, eight of the highest 100 peaks in Colorado don't have names and more than 100 of the 608 peaks over 13,000 feet remain nameless. What names there are, however, provide valuable clues to the way humans view the mountains—honoring our heroes, giving form to our fears, and shaping our dreams.

MOSQUITO RANGE—for an insect which landed on the application form for one of the first mining claims in the area.

MOUNT SNEFFELS (San Juans)—after Snaefell Mountain in *Journey to the Center of the Earth* by Jules Verne.

MOUNT AETNA (Sawatch)—from "etna," the mountain of rubble in which the Greek god Zeus buried a flame-breathing monster named Typhon.

SANGRE DE CRISTO RANGE—from a Spanish priest who saw the deep red sunset reflecting over the peaks from the San Luis Valley and exclaimed "Sangre de Cristo" or "the blood of Christ."

TEOCALLI MOUNTAIN (Elk)—given to the peak by the Hayden Survey for the resemblance of its silhouette to pyramids worshipped by the Aztecs.

PACIFIC PEAK (Tenmile)—for its position just west of the Continental Divide which makes its creeks flow to the Pacific Ocean.

GIANTTRACK MOUNTAIN (Front)—deep potholes six to eight feet deep worn by uneven erosion on the summit looked to Arapaho Indians like the footprints of a giant.

JACKSTRAW MOUNTAIN (Never Summer)—a fire in 1872 left the mountain strewn with the charred spires of lodgepole pine.

NEVER SUMMER RANGE—called "Ni-chebe-chii" by the Arapaho, the No Never Summer Mountains.

MOUNT EOLUS (San Juan)—for Aeolus, the Greek god of the winds, by the Hayden Survey Party.

GOTHIC MOUNTAIN (Elk)—the face of the peak carved into enormous pillars reminded miners of Gothic architecture.

TEDDY PEAK (Culebra)—for Teddy Roosevelt, who hunted in the area.

CULEBRA RANGE—Spanish for "snake."

GORE RANGE—for Sir George Gore, who hunted the area in 1855 with Jim Bridger as a guide. One of only two ranges in Colorado named after a person who was not a saint.

LA PLATA PEAK (Sawatch)—Spanish for "silver."

MOUNT SHAVANO (Sawatch)—for the leader of one band of Mountain Utes.

EUREKA MOUNTAIN (Sangre de Cristo)—the exclaimation of a lucky miner who struck it rich at the base of the peak.

NECKLACE PEAK (Gore Range)—for the string of jewel-like lakes which surround it.

BYERS PEAK (Front)—for the mountain-climbing newspaper man William Byers, who scaled many Colorado peaks and reported his adventures in the newspaper he founded, the *Rocky Mountain News.*

LONE EAGLE PEAK (Front)—for the nickname of Charles Lindbergh, first to fly an airplane across the Atlantic Ocean.

MOUNT YPSILON (Mummy)—wears its name on its face with a snow- filled "Y" across its cliffs. The name is the Greek word for the letter "Y."

HUMBOLDT PEAK (Sangre de Cristo)—for the explorer, mountaineer, writer, and scientist Alexander von Humboldt.

SAWATCH RANGE—Indian for "waters of the blue earth."

ROCKY MOUNTAINS—called "the Shining Mountains" by early Indians, the "Stony Mountains" by President Jefferson, and finally the "Rocky Mountains" by Lewis and Clark.

Winter frosts the Sangre de Cristo Range in purple hues, above. DAVID MUENCH

Page 126: Molas Lake mirrors the Grenadier Range. DAVID MUENCH

Page 127: A blazing campfire sends sparks into the twilight sky between Grays and Torrys peaks in the Front Range. STEPHEN TRIMBLE

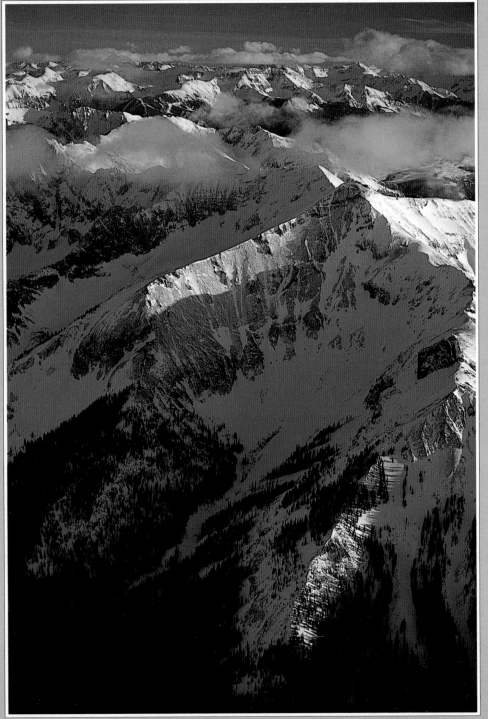

There is an endlessness about mountains
the sight of the Colorado Rockies under the sun,
the blues of day sky
the grays of night sky
mingling together at sunset
like dark water,
light flowing through a pass as if
through a door ajar.

Out to the horizons
the peaks seem to settle
like waves after a storm
or a song that fades to silence.

PHOTO BY TOM TILL